Innovation in Teaching of Research Methodology Excellence Awards 2019

An Anthology of Case Histories

Edited by Dan Remenyi

Innovation in the Teaching of Research Methodology Excellence Awards 2019: An Anthology of Case Histories

ISBN: 978-1-912764-26-6

Published by: Academic Conferences and Publishing International Limited, Reading, RG4 9SJ, United Kingdom, info@academic-conferences.org

Available from www.academic-bookshop.com

Table of Contents

Acknowledgements

We would like to thank the judges, who initially read the abstracts of the case histories submitted to the competition and discussed these to select those to be submitted as full case histories. They subsequently evaluated the entries and made further selections to produce the finalists who are represented in this book.

Judging Team

Dr. Shawren Singh is a senior lecturer in the School of Computing at the University of South Africa and has spent more than 15 years teaching and researching in the Information Systems space. His research has focused on e-Government and the postgraduate research experience. His research has been published internationally and he has presented papers at several conferences. He is also supervising several postgraduate candidates. His current academic research interests are in information systems, including methods evaluating mobile applications.

Mark Saunders is Professor of Business Research Methods at the Birmingham Business School and College of Social Sciences Director of Postgraduate Research Methods Training at the University of Birmingham. He also holds visiting professorships at the Universities of Malta, Surrey and Worcester and is a Fellow of the British Academy of Management. His research interests include research methods and in particular participant selection and methods for understanding organizational relationships; human resource aspects of the management of change, in particular trust within and between organizations and organizational learning; and small and medium sized enterprise (SME) success. Mark has a long-term interest in teaching research methods, doctoral training and supervison. He has also organised a range of doctoral summer schools, symposia and colloquia for a number of organisations, including the British Academy of

Management and the University Forum for Human Resources Development.

Marie Ashwin joined EM Normandie in 2008 as Professor of Marketing and Management after two decades of international experience. Since 2011 she has been Dissertation Coordinator adding an additional cultural dimension to her work enhancing the standing of RM amongst staff and students, and adding value to the teaching of methodology.

Introduction

The Innovation in the Teaching of Research Methods Excellence Awards is being run for the 5th time this year.

We continue to be encouraged by the interest which has been shown in these Excellence Awards, as we believe that the case histories recorded here are a valuable asset to those who are trying to improve their teaching of research methodology in the social sciences.

Initially 20 submissions were received and 15 contenders were invited to submit a full case history describing their initiative. These case histories were double-blind peer review and this publication contains the entries of the shortlisted contestants. We are once again pleased to see the global reach these Awards have with contributions this year from Belgium, New Zealand, Netherlands, Portugal and South Africa.

We feel that these case histories provide helpful insights into the types of issues academics are coping with when teaching research methodology today in various parts of the world.

These case histories are also included in a compilation book of the past five years Excellence Awards finalists.

Dan Remenyi
Editor
June 2019
dan.remenyi@academic-publishing.org

Research in a Practice: Preparing Students for Real Research Publications

Manuel Au-Yong-Oliveira[1], Frederico Branco[2], José Martins[2] and Ramiro Gonçalves[2]
[1]GOVCOPP, Department of Economics, Management, Industrial Engineering and Tourism, University of Aveiro, Portugal
[2]INESC TEC and University of Trás-os-Montes and Alto Douro, Vila Real, Portugal
mao@ua.pt
fbranco@utad.pt
jmartins@utad.pt
ramiro@utad.pt

1. Introduction

Research involves answering an intellectual question and as such academic research "follows to some extent a formal procedure [...] a research design, the collection of data or evidence, the analysis of the data and the reaching of a conclusion [...] There is a high degree of flexibility as to how these processes are actually performed" (Remenyi, 2017, p.189). In my classes a broad theme is considered, within which students must perform research. However, students are given considerable freedom in the final choice of their specific research topic and on how they intend to answer the research question(s) – the "voyage of discovery" (Saunders and Lewis, 2018, p.1) on which they wish to embark.

I have only this year started to lecture on doctoral courses and so the knowledge shared herein pertains to Master's degree lecturing efforts. To date I have not focused on publishing with undergraduate students, though it is an objective of mine to change this soon.

In Master's degree classes I always give two options through which to pass my subjects – classes on Strategy and Competitiveness or on the Management of Innovation and Technology – and these are to do a final

1

exam worth 100% of the grade; or to write an academic article good enough for publication worth 50% of the grade in addition to doing a test worth the remaining 50% of the grade. The vast majority of students choose the latter (my class in Strategy and Competitiveness this first semester of 2018-2019 had a total of 167 students and 121 chose to write the academic article plus do a test).

I am clear in that the best articles will be chosen for submission and possible publication in top academic conferences (indexed in databases such as Scopus and ISI Web of Science) where the articles will be subject first to double blind peer review – and thus an analysis and evaluation by a panel independent of the lecturer.

Students have reacted very well to this challenge and in 2017-2018, in my Management of Innovation and Technology class, I as the lecturer was evaluated for my global performance by students with an average of 7.78 out of a possible 9 points (at the end of the semester and as a part of our Quality Assurance System at the University of Aveiro). That semester a total of twelve academic papers were successfully submitted (with Master's students) and published in the proceedings of the ECIE 2018 (13th European Conference on Innovation and Entrepreneurship), held at the University of Aveiro (two more papers were published with research students). This first semester of 2018-2019, a total of 15 papers have already been published (in English) in the WorldCist 2019 Springer book series and conference proceedings (7th World Conference on Information Systems and Technologies, La Toja Island, Spain); one will be published in the ECIE 2019 (14th European Conference on Innovation and Entrepreneurship, Kalamata, Greece); and an additional three papers have been accepted for publication at the CISTI 2019 (14th Iberian Conference on Information Systems and Technologies, Coimbra, Portugal) – in Portuguese. The course which originated this latter publication effort was the Strategy and Competitiveness Master's degree course, mentioned above, and for which I had a general average of 7.72 out of a possible 9 points (at the end of the semester and again as a part of our Quality Assurance System at the University of Aveiro). This is considered to be quite good as I was, in this case, potentially evaluated by a public of 167 students (a total of 82 students actually filled in the feedback forms). To give readers an idea of the publication rate for the Strategy and Competitiveness Master's degree course, a total of 37 student groups

2

submitted course work and 19 of these will be published in three international ISI Web of Science / Scopus conferences – which is 51.4%, or just over half of them. The quality of the student work that semester was quite exceptional.

Students are first coached on the research design and on the field method they want to follow for their academic research – interviews, focus groups and / or questionnaires (see Remenyi, 2013, for a discussion of these).

Students will then tend to do a mix of these, to gather primary data for their coursework essays.

Publishing may occur in academic conferences, scientific journals, or in books. In fact, over the years we have successfully published with students in all of these outlets. Students react very well to the objective of having their work published. Plagiarism, once a "disease" plaguing us, has practically been eradicated, as students understand that they need to be original when we are talking about getting their work published.

Students are encouraged to follow a research design and to solve a research problem, to do field work after fine-tuning their research instruments, such as an interview script or a questionnaire, and they are further encouraged to validate their research results and to make a contribution – however small – to theory and to practitioners. Primary and secondary data, samples, data saturation, data triangulation, parsimony, and peer review (as well as actually following the suggestions given by anonymous reviewers) are new terms which students learn about in practice and actually apply in the research process which they undergo – rather than just learning about them in overhead slides and in a classroom presentation.

2. The infrastructure

This teaching process has been very satisfactory and we have strong support for my teaching methods by the Head of my Department (DEGEIT), Professor Carlos Costa, whom I consider to be a visionary. I am also very grateful to my research institution, GOVCOPP, for finance provided.

I am additionally very grateful to my team of three colleagues (who are co-authors of this book chapter) who have given me second opinions on

3

student work and who have helped improve the work submitted, for publication purposes, as well as also helping with finance (from their research entities, as well as from other sources), especially this last semester – for the publication of such work in international academic conferences. Top international conferences tend to be quite expensive and out of the reach of Portuguese students and it is thus a major task to find funding. Students are, however, given the option to publish by themselves, if they wish, without lecturers as co-authors.

I communicate with the students mainly via e-mail, but also via Messenger and WhatsApp. I also use my smartphone for voice communication. There is, however, no replacement for face-to-face meetings on the research efforts, which happen in class and after class too.

All classrooms at the University of Aveiro have Internet Wi Fi. We also have colour video / slide projectors in each classroom. Each subject has an e-learning platform on which to put course material and discussions may also be had online through the e-learning forum functionality. These are all very useful tools to have at our disposal.

3. The challenges

It is a challenge to get students to write their coursework in English. Students who have studied languages at the university level definitely have an advantage over those who have come into contact with foreign languages, including English, only in secondary school and perhaps before that. All student manuscripts written in English (and if the content is at the standard we believe to be acceptable for publication) are reviewed by myself, a native English speaker, and/or by a professional English language reviewer. We do also submit student work written in Portuguese (by students not comfortable with the English language) to certain international conferences which accept papers written in Portuguese (e.g. the CISTI 2019, as mentioned above), and the offering of such events is indeed increasing over time, as is their quality.

Of note is that the motivation level tends to be very high when I as a lecturer state that international publications (indexed in major international databases, and/or part of a book series, with peer-review, such as those by Springer) will possibly lead to better starting salaries as employers will perceive that students who have published their work will be proficient at writing reports and when working as team members (the assignments are group efforts of up to four students each).

Another challenge pertains to the conference itself. We tend to choose a topic for the semester (e.g. innovation and entrepreneurship, or technology) and then choose a conference in this area of expertise. We want to choose a conference we can submit manuscripts to during the semester (say, mid-way through the semester) and hopefully one which will also give feedback on the work submitted before the semester ends, so that the students can see the full loop of the publishing process. We also generally choose conferences that are close by to the University of Aveiro and which students may travel to if they wish, to present their work (the ECIE 2018 worked perfectly as it was held at the University of Aveiro).

Time is obviously of essence, as I need to first give students training on research methods, while also providing new knowledge on the subject / topic chosen for the semester; then I have to give them enough time to do their field research and to write a paper; and then, finally, I have to correct the group work in time for submittal to the venue. If I receive 37 group projects (as I did for Strategy and Competitiveness, in 2018-2019 – 23 in English and 14 in Portuguese) it will take me two months of non-stop work to correct them. Students are then informed of the shortcomings of their papers and are challenged to improve on them. Most agree to improve on their work. Marks are awarded to the student papers according to what they turn out to be, in the end, and not according to how they were first received by the lecturer. The student corrections normally involve: 1) reinforcing the literature review with more references (as students tend to perhaps perform a rather superficial literature review) and in particular from peer review sources, such as the Scopus database (students often use blogs and other media outlets – some of which are better than others); 2) reviewing the literature critically and developing "a clear argument to contextualise and justify" the research (Saunders and Lewis, 2018, p.32), rather than just listing references and definitions; 3) making the methodology section more academic and professional, including details about the interviewing and sampling done for the paper (especially, in this latter case, if a survey was performed); 4) presenting the results of the field research in a scientific manner; for example, in the case of interviews performed, including quotes from the interviews in a table and according to a topic or code found in the data; 5) correcting the references section, as students tend not to closely adhere to the reference style required by the venue; 6) focusing on the original contribution of the article to the literature and for practitioners; 7) generally ensuring that the objectives of the research effort were achieved.

Another challenge is to obviously get as many students to publish their work as possible. This will involve getting the standard of their work up to the necessary level. For the Strategy and Competitiveness Master's degree course, mentioned above, out of 167 students, 121 submitted course work; and out of these, 68 students will have their work published (40.7% of the class and 56.2% of those who submitted course work). Of the students who will publish their work, 100% will publish internationally for the first time.

4. How the initiative was received by the users or participants

The student work which is submitted for double-blind peer review at an international conference leads to a number of useful comments shared with the students, which is very useful for students to understand how they may improve on their work. Rarely do I receive a comment such as "Professor, there are too many things which need to be changed, and we simply do not have the time to do the changes, as we are in the middle of our exam period". If such an answer is received and if we think that the article is worth it we may proceed to do the changes ourselves. Sometimes, though, the article will be dropped from the conference. Erasmus students tend to not be so keen on publishing their work, though some do want to go through the process. Overall, students are very excited to get their work published.

E-mails received from students include the following: "We thank you for your incentive and help. We are very happy with the final result." I do in fact encourage students to submit course work with the ambition of getting it published as this is seen to be so much more worthwhile than just doing an exam to pass the subject; or doing course work which will be forgotten in a drawer. Students tend to be ecstatic when their work is accepted for publication, as this quote by students shows: "We are very happy! The group accepts all of the alterations [which you have done] and sincerely thanks all of the accompaniment." I do actually get actively involved in the improving of the articles and act as a type of "research coach" along the publication process, which the students appreciate. Students do often state that they have never before thought of getting their work published. The research rules which I teach are for the most part entirely new to the vast majority of my Master's students.

Some students may have queries on how to proceed after receiving the reviewer comments. For example, one group of students stated: "First of all we thank you for the news on the acceptance of our article. We have discussed the issue as a group and we have some queries in relation to the alterations requested. We would like to know if we may schedule a meeting with you in order to know your opinion. The meeting could be via Skype, if you prefer. In any case, we are going to carefully re-read and analyse the article again. We thank you once again for your attention and availability." A degree of perfectionism is present in most students, who want their article to be "just perfect". Thus, the lecturer who has a lot of experience publishing at this level (and higher, in peer-review indexed journals) is welcomed as being very necessary. Students do also tend to come in groups, with as many of the group members as possible, to meet with the lecturer. In my experience students do share knowledge and feedback given, amongst themselves, very well. Albeit, I do send feedback to all of the e-mails of the group members, to ensure that all are aware of what is happening.

5. The learning outcomes

"The final purpose of all research is to learn and in so doing add something of value to the body of theoretical and practical knowledge" (Remenyi, 2017, p.121)

Very useful reviewer feedback will include comments such as those below, which is essential to the learning process. "The research process itself teaches the researcher as he or she moves from step to step sometimes in a cycle of improvement" (Remenyi, 2017, p.121). There is not currently much written about the peer-review publication process in major manuals on research methodology and so students are, for the most part, "in the dark" about how to proceed (see for example Saunders et al., 2016; and Saunders and Lewis, 2018).

Examples of positive reviewer comments received by student groups:

- "The authors are to be commended for their efforts in being able to receive 1,661 answers to their survey. Of note is that the respondents are very international and are also very interested in the subject. The contributions of the article are of interest to practitioners and to academics alike."

- "The paper complies with the scientific writing protocols, and with the rules of the call. The subject investigated is relevant and of interest to the academic community. The results can lead to applications in schools and educational centers."

- "The topic of the article is very interesting. The structure is well written and it also presents an appropriate methodology. In my opinion this article should be accepted without restrictions. Good work!"

- "The comparison between Farfetch and Josefinas regarding digital marketing is a good idea. Consider my suggesting, for future research, a comparison between Josefinas and other women shoe brands that do not rely so much on social media and also have physical stores."

Examples of more "negative" reviewer comments received – students at times need to be mature enough to deal with what is seen to be constructive criticism:

- "The article needs to be reinforced with more recent and academic references. The authors should also indicate what questions were asked in the survey."

- "The research questions were not set specifically and as a result, the author's inferences are interesting but not focused enough."

- "The introduction section, at the end, should include a paragraph that presents the remaining sections of the manuscript."

- "You followed a mixed methodology. In the methodology section the phrase "This questionnaire, which was placed online and disseminated through social media and through our classmates, was answered by 66 people (a total of 56 valid responses were received)" should be rewritten in order to clarify who answered the questionnaire and in what form. The table referring to the profile of the interviewees should omit the interviewees' names, and names can be replaced by interviewee 1, interviewee 2, etc. Review, in accordance with the table, the citation of each interviewee in the latter sections."

- "The topic is interesting and is in the tracks of the conference. However, it is not clear what the innovative aspects of the paper are. There is no related work section. There are some studies about the impact of ICT on elder people that have not been considered. The article needs a systematic literature review in order to determine the novel aspects of the solution provided. ICT must be analysed not only from the age aspects but focusing on other elements like culture and socioeconomic issues."

- "It would be interesting to add data that give rigor to the comments like: "Portugal is an old country filled with old people", as in this way value is given to the objective of the article."

- "With respect to recommendations the authors should also explain how would they intend to deal with the evaluation of how employees react to the possibility of working with virtual assistants side-by-side. What is proposed? Using the collaboration of Altice Labs?"

- "The authors only present a very light analysis of some "not so scientific" literature and fail in creating a valid contribution to other researchers and to organizations that are planning on implementing Industry 4.0 solutions."

- "The Discussion section should be revised and further extended by presenting a set of considerations on the alignment between the achieved results and the existing literature."

On the Quality Assurance System at the University of Aveiro, which measures the success of each course, at the end of each semester; for Strategy and Competitiveness (Master's level), lectured this first semester of 2018-2019 (to 167 students), some of the average grades in the student survey awarded to Manuel Au-Yong Oliveira, by the students, were (scale of 1-9, very low to very high):

- Global evaluation of the performance of the lecturer: 7.8
- Relationship between the lecturer and the student: 7.82
- Mastery of the course content: 7.96
- Availability of the lecturer to see students after class: 8.07

These grades were the best given by students, on the Master's degree in Management, out of all of the courses in the first year (the Master's degree in Management, at the University of Aveiro, is a two-year course) and for the first semester of 2018-2019. The Strategy and Competitiveness course actually had students from a number of different backgrounds, as the course is available as an option to various Master's degrees at the University of Aveiro (Master's degrees such as in Management, Economics, Physics Engineering, Engineering and Industrial Management, Languages and Corporate Relations, Electronics and Telecommunications Engineering, and Informatics Engineering).

6. Plans to further develop the initiative

"In the context of research the word 'network' refers to a group of people or institutions which have a shared interest in the research being conducted" (Remenyi, 2017, p.145)

We plan in future to continue to get student work published, as this is in accordance with the higher education objectives of our universities, as well as in the country as a whole. However, finance is a problem, and a degree of sacrifice and/or ingeniousness is at times required. Working in a network has made our results achieved so far possible. Working alone would simply mean that such an initiative would not be possible. In future, we hope to coach students well enough for them to be able to also publish articles more regularly in peer-review research journals (see for example Au-Yong-Oliveira et al., 2017, for an example of this). This is also more highly valued by the academic community. Another alternative is editing books with chapters co-authored by students, which we have also done in the past, and which also works out as being more economical (see for example Au-Yong-Oliveira et al., 2016; and Au-Yong-Oliveira and Gonçalves, 2017).

The problem with the latter is that without external and independent reviewers there is more risk and work involved in the review process (we have to do all the work ourselves). Additionally, we would also like to organize another major conference at the University of Aveiro – preferably indexed in Scopus and ISI Web of Science (see for example Costa et al., 2018 – the proceedings book for the ECIE 2018).

As stated above, it is an objective to get undergraduate students to publish internationally, too, in the short term. This will present itself with other unique challenges and perhaps less students, in relation to the whole class, will be able to do so.

As regards ethics in publishing, the student work, if seen to be suspect, is put through the Google search engine to check for plagiarism. More recently, a specific software tool for that end has been adopted by the University of Aveiro and been made available to lecturers – Urkund. I intend to use this more often in the future. However, no serious or even moderately serious situations have been detected since the publishing process challenge has been instituted in class. This may also be due to the fact that a comprehensive training session on how to avoid plagiarism is administered to students at the very start of the semester. Such efforts are to continue.

References

Au-Yong Oliveira, M., Gonçalves, R., Martins, J., Moreira, F., Branco, F. (Editors) (2016). Casos de estudo em estratégia e marketing: Promovendo o debate empresarial. [Case studies in strategy and marketing: Promoting the corporate debate] Faro, Portugal: Sílabas & Desafios.

Au-Yong Oliveira, M., Gonçalves, R. (Editors) (2017). Estratégia, inovação e mudança – Casos de estudo sobre competitividade / Strategy, innovation and change: case studies on competitiveness. Aveiro, Portugal: UA Editora.

Au-Yong-Oliveira, M., Reis de Sousa, R.J., Gonçalves, R. (2017). Cultural differences still matter: Adapting products and positioning for international success. Journal on Advances in Theoretical and Applied Informatics (JADI), Vol. 3(1), pp.103-110.

Costa, C., Au-Yong-Oliveira, M., Amorim, M. (Editors) (2018). Proceedings of the 13th European Conference on Innovation and Entrepreneurship, ECIE 2018, University of Aveiro, 20-21 September.

Remenyi, D. (2013). Field methods for academic research – Interviews, focus groups & questionnaires. 3rd edition. Reading, UK: ACPIL.

Remenyi, D. (2017). Dictionary of research concepts and issues. 2nd edition. Reading, UK: ACPIL.

Saunders, M., Lewis, P. (2018). Doing research in business and management. 2nd edition. Harlow, UK: Pearson.

Saunders, M., Lewis, P., Thornhill, A. (2016). Research methods for business students. 7th edition. Harlow, UK: Pearson.

Author Biographies

Manuel Au-Yong Oliveira is an Assistant Professor at the University of Aveiro (Department of Economics, Management, Industrial Engineering and Tourism – DEGEIT), in Portugal, where he lectures at the undergraduate, master's and doctoral levels on marketing, strategy, innovation, technology and on research methods. At present, Manuel is the Director of the Master's Degree in Management at the University of Aveiro. Manuel is also a member of the Executive Committee of his department - DEGEIT - University of Aveiro. Manuel has a passion for teaching and education.

Frederico Branco is an Assistant Professor at the University of Trás-os-Montes and Alto Douro and a Senior Research at INESC TEC. He has published over 50 articles in journals and event proceedings and participates continuously in a number of research projects. His professional career is also directly related with industry, with a particular focus on various planning and implementation projects of Information Systems, in the agri-food and services sectors. Frederico currently holds several senior management functions in the areas of Operations, Information Systems and Quality Management.

José Martins is currently an Invited Assistant Professor at the University of Trás-os-Montes and Alto Douro, an Invited Assistant Professor at the Polytechnic Institute of Bragança and a Senior Researcher at INESC TEC. He has published over 90 articles in indexed journals and event proceedings focusing on the Information Systems and Human-Computer

Interaction topics. During his professional career José has also worked as an information systems and technologies senior consultant where he directly participated in several international projects.

Ramiro Gonçalves is an Associate Professor with Habilitation at the University of Trás-os-Montes e Alto Douro, in Vila Real, Portugal, and a Senior Researcher at INESC TEC Associated Laboratory, in Porto, Portugal. Ramiro has around 200 publications (including book chapters, Scientific Citation Index journal articles, as well as publications in refereed conference proceedings). Ramiro has also been linked to industry throughout his career, and more recently as a senior manager in the public sector.

Beyond Fiction and Science: Using Stories, Movies and Games to Teach Qualitative Research

Dr. Lakshmi Balachandran Nair
Assistant Professor (Senior), Methodology and Statistics Department,
Utrecht University, Utrecht, the Netherlands
l.balachandrannair@uu.nl

Abstract : This initiative involves multiple activities which use popular media to teach qualitative research. Here I present one such activity - two short scenes from the movie "The circle" are used to discuss qualitative data collection ethics.

1. Context

Prior research has explored the importance of popular media in researching (e.g.: Kara, 2003) and teaching contextual topics in fields ranging from law (Caron, 2002) to sustainability (Moezzi et al., 2017). Inspired by these attempts, I am developing an initiative for teaching qualitative methodological topics using popular media. The context of my teaching initiative is qualitative methodology courses for Bachelor and Masters students from social science disciplines (education, management, psychology etc.). So far I have experimented with media such as stories (e.g.: Harry Potter), games (e.g.: Her Story), commercials (e.g.: Dove), and movies (e.g.: The circle) to explain various facets of qualitative research. The Harry Potter and Her Story activities have been converted into teaching case studies which are accepted for publication in Sage Business Cases forthcoming in January 2020 (Nair, In press – a & b).

2. Using popular media to teach qualitative research

Saldaña (2009) recognized the use of popular films as pedagogical tools for qualitative research. Movie scenes, commercials, and TV programs have immense instructional potential. Likewise, stories and novels allow us to explicate, interpret, and build persuasive arguments (Bruner, 1990; Gudmundsdottir, 1991; Jonassen and Hernandez-Serrano, 2002). Since students often perceive methodology courses as difficult, introducing qualitative research concepts through dry lectures will not ensure the effective fulfillment of course objectives. Experiences in narrative forms (as presented by popular media) require less cognitive effort to understand than traditional lectures (Jonassen and Hernandez-Serrano, 2002). Therefore, incorporating popular media techniques into teaching contributes to more enthusiasm and engagement from the students as well as their thorough and clearer understanding. Indeed, there are not many instructional popular media focusing specifically on qualitative methodology (Saldaña, 2009). But even non-instructional popular media, regardless of their original intent, has the potential to fill this pedagogical gap. This is the core idea behind this initiative.

2.1 Objectives of the teaching initiative

The general objective of this teaching initiative is to use popular media as a tool for introducing students to the general features of qualitative research (points 1-5 below). Subsequently, the initiative also facilitates critical thinking about said features.

1. Research questions, research design, and sampling
2. Data collection
3. Data analysis
4. Reporting and quality check
5. Ethical considerations

3. Infrastructure

This initiative requires only a computer with internet connection, a projector, and/or printed copies of the mediums being used.

4. Challenges

One potential challenge involves copyright laws. However, I always make certain that the activities are within the legally allowed fair use. Fair use is an exception to the right of copyright users under specific circumstances where the use constitutes predominant cultural or social benefits (Section 107 of U.S. copyright law; Adler et al., 2012). To ensure ethical usage of media, I include relevant citations in my teaching material and power point slides. Furthermore, while preparing teaching case studies which require the complete story/game to be included in the case, I contact the copyright holders and receive their written permission.

For instance, in this proposal I use the specific example of one activity in the teaching initiative. I employ two short (4-5 minutes long) scenes from the movie "The circle" to teach the topic of ethics in qualitative data collection. The videos of both these scenes are freely available in YouTube (Emma Watson Screamed After Ellar Coltrane's Death - The Circle, 2018; Patel, 2017). Furthermore, since the material is utilized for teaching and scholarship (i.e. nonprofit, educational purposes), it constitutes fair use. The use is transformative, i.e. the movie scenes are employed in a new context, different from the intended uses in the original movie. I give more details of the activity below.

4.1   Sample activity: Movie
"The circle" (Year of release: 2017; Director: James Ponsoldt)

Length of activity: 30 minutes

Level: 2nd and 3rd year Bachelor students

Objectives: To introduce students to ethical perspectives and ethical issues in

                                       qualitative data collection;

                                       To facilitate critical thinking about the ethicality of qualitative data

                                       collection in a specific situation;

                                       To facilitate critical thinking about ethical perspectives and issues in

                                       students' own qualitative research projects

5. Activity
The activity I describe here involves the techno-thriller movie 'The circle' (Bregman et al., 2017). I use this activity for teaching students about ethical considerations in qualitative data collection. Specifically, the activity addresses some of the most common ethical issues in qualitative data collection as well as three theoretical perspectives on ethics - Universalism (deontological approach), Utilitarianism (teleological approach), and Situational (principled) relativism (Eriksson and Kovalainen, 2016; Ritchie et al., 2013). Table 1 gives a summary.

Table 1: Ethical issues and perspectives in qualitative data collection

ETHICS IN QUALITATIVE DATA COLLECTION	Issues	Unreasonable demands on participants or researchers, Lack of informed consent, Involuntary participation through coercion, No communication regarding risks of harm, Lack of confidentiality and anonymity, Mishandling environmental and emotive risks, Problems related to sponsor-researcher relationship
	Perspectives	Universalism (deontological approach), Utilitarianism (teleological approach), Situational (principled) relativism

The movie (Bergman et al., 2017; IMDb, 2017) portrays a timely theme – privacy and accountability in the social media era. In the movie, "The circle" is a social media company. The main characters in the movie are Mae Holland (played by Emma Watson) - an employee of The circle, Eamon Bailey (played by Tom Hanks) - the CEO, and Mercer Regalado (Ellar Coltrane) - a friend of Mae's. I use two specific scenes from this movie to explain and evoke critical discussions on ethics in qualitative data collection.

The first scene shows Mae in a company-wide meeting, demonstrating the power of the so-called "Soul Search" program developed by The circle. This scene is available in YouTube: https://www.youtube.com/watch?v=Mro9RCAhvE4 (Patel, 2017; Bergman et al., 2017).

In this scene, Mae along with her audience (other employees of The circle) tests Soul Search by attempting to detect an escaped prisoner. The computer randomly selects a fugitive named Fiona Highbridge who was convicted of killing her three children by starving them. The users of the Soul Search program identify and get her arrested within 10 minutes. The users, Mae, and the audience are happy with the results.

The second scene shows Mae being insisted on by her boss and the audience to detect her friend Mercer. This scene is also in YouTube: https://www.youtube.com/watch?v=WLG_H9Tba9A (Bergman et al., 2017; Emma Watson Screamed After Ellar Coltrane's Death - The Circle). Unwillingly, Mae goes ahead with the demand. The users find Mercer also quite quickly, in an isolated cabin where he is working on making chandeliers. The users taunt him. Mercer, who is agitated by the users and the cameras, tries to drive away in his truck. Unfortunately, he crashes into a bridge, falls off, and dies.

After the students watch these video clips, they discuss the ethical considerations at play in both the situations (see Table 1). The questions below facilitate this discussion. Potential answers to these questions are included below them.

6. Questions & answers

6.1   What ethical issues are involved in the two scenes?

In both scenes, there is lack of informed consent. Neither Fiona nor Mercer gave their permission to be traced down. In the second scene, the audience and her boss are being unreasonably demanding on Mae. It is very clear that Mae is not happy to use Soul Search to locate her friend Mercer. However, Mae's boss and colleagues disregard her obvious discomfort and force her to conduct the search.

Likewise, Mercer does not want to be found. But the program users are invading his privacy. Fiona, Mae, and Mercer did not give their consent to be part of the program testing. Mae is coerced to locate the other two, Mercer and Fiona are coerced to be in the public eye. The private information (whereabouts) of both Mercer and Fiona are made public. None of the three parties are made aware of the risks of harm involved. Due to this unethical search procedure, Mercer is subjected to emotional harm and subsequent death, Fiona is arrested, and Mae is under emotional distress. The audience and the public are still unaware of the harms involved.

6.2   How are these ethical issues related to qualitative data collection?

The ethical issues we notice in the two scenes of the movie are also parallel with those in qualitative data collection. The explanations are included below (Nair, In press - a).

1. Problems related to sponsor-researcher relationship – Sponsorship of research by companies or organizations do not create any issues as long as the sponsorship contract is constructed ethically and mutually beneficially. However, in some cases, constructing the contract ethically might be difficult. The sponsor organization might insist that the researcher should comply with some of its demands. For instance, the researcher might be asked to collect and analyze data which puts the organization in a good light. Likewise, the organization might not be interested in disseminating results which affect its publicity. Not unlike movie scene 2, in which Mae's boss coerces her to find Mercer, the researcher might sometimes choose to comply with the funding organization's demands just to ensure the sponsorship continues.

2. Unreasonable demands on participants or researchers – The research should be reasonable for both the participants and the researchers. Reasonable research involves ensuring physical, psychological, and social wellbeing of the participants as well as the researcher. Furthermore, the researcher should ensure that the time and effort put in by the participant is acknowledged and when applicable, compensated. In the scenes we watched, unreasonable demands are made on Mae, Mercer, and Fiona. Furthermore, the program users are also being subjected to unreasonable demands (albeit more incidentally). By asking them to track down a known criminal (in scene 1), the company is putting them in danger.

3. Lack of informed consent – Ideally, a researcher should receive informed consent from the participants before data collection. This involves providing the participants information about the research objectives, data use and management, confidentiality and anonymity, as well as any potential harms involved in a particular study. Once the participants have all this information, they are able to make decisions about their participation. Lack of informed consent thereby prevents the participant from making informed decisions. In the two scenes we watched, no informed consent was collected from the program users, Mae, Mercer, or Fiona.

4. Involuntary participation through coercion – In some cases, the participants are not given a chance to make an informed decision.

20

Regardless of their interest in participating, they are coerced to participate through the use of social or employment expectations. For instance, an employee of a company might be coerced to participate in a focus group discussion approved by his project manager just out of job security concerns. This is analogous to how Mae was coerced to track Mercer.

5. Lack of confidentiality and anonymity – The researcher should ensure that all the data is anonymized, by giving participants code names or pseudonyms. Likewise, the collected data should be stored confidentially. The consent regarding data storage should be periodically reaffirmed, especially in the context of studies involving children (who might change their mind about consenting once they grow up). This resembles what is happening in the two movie scenarios. Soul Search reveals the identity and whereabouts of Fiona and Mercer to the audience and the program users, thereby violating the confidentiality and anonymity rights of the former.

6. Mishandling environmental and emotive risks – For ensuring the researcher's safety, risk assessment should be performed before collecting data from unsafe environments. The researchers should also receive safe transportation and keep formal records of the specific places where they are collecting data. In the case of emotive risks, the researcher should be given an opportunity to withdraw or limit data collection encounters. Proper awareness of the involved risks should be provided. The researchers who are feeling guilt, anger, frustration, or trauma due to the data collection process should receive adequate peer support. In the movie, Mae experienced guilt and trauma due to the Soul Search experiment. Ideally, The Circle should facilitate her recovery and reintegration.

7. How would you compare the ethical issues in scene 1 and 2? Is the researcher/ circle unethical in both scenes? Substantiate your answers.

Here, students are asked to compare the ethicality of the two scenes. Once the students answer, the teacher can use the answers to introduce three ethical perspectives (Nair, In press - a; Ritchie et al., 2013). Some students might argue that scene 1 is ethical since it used Soul Search program to capture a criminal. This approach is part of the Utilitarian (teleological) ethical perspective. According to this perspective, decisions made should be based on consequences of a particular action. The benefits and drawbacks of the action should be measured and the decision leading to the best outcome should be chosen. In scene 1, users of Soul Search program found Fiona. As per Utilitarian perspective, this action is ethical since the benefit of the action is capturing a criminal who was hiding from law.

Others students might say the action is unethical, since the criminal's privacy and confidentiality are broken and that matters, despite her criminal activities. This approach is known as Universalism or deontological approach. Under this perspective, ethical rules are meant to be never broken. Regardless of the involved situation, the rules should always remain the same. Since privacy and confidentiality are ethical considerations, even Fiona deserves them.

Similarly, another potential approach to this situation is a case by case approach. Fiona, as a criminal, is tracked down using the Soul Search program. Another criminal might not be, since the situation in hand might suggest otherwise. For instance, let us assume that after her capture Fiona is imprisoned for life. One might imagine every criminal who is captured would face the same fate. However, if we follow the situational ethics perspective, decision making takes a case by case approach. For instance, imagine Frank Abagnale Jr., the conman from "Catch Me If You Can" (Spielberg, 2002) is captured instead of Fiona. Situational ethics would suggest that Mr. Abagnale Jr., being a brilliant conman who knows how conmen work, should be given a job at the FBI bank fraud department instead of being imprisoned.

After this discussion, the students should be asked to consider their own specific research projects. They have to come up with a plan to ensure ethical data collection. They also have to elaborate upon their chosen ethical perspective.

8. Reception by users

As of now, I am still in the process of developing this initiative by experimenting with different activities. So far I have used different activities from this initiative for the course "Qualitative Inquiry in Everyday

Life" (7.5 ECTS Bachelor course at University College Utrecht; Course period = August to December 2018; Maximum capacity = 28 students).

Students of this course are very receptive to the activities involved. During student evaluation (January 2019), this course received 3.5 out of 5 points. Although specific questions regarding this teaching initiative are not yet included in the evaluation form, students praised the relevance and teaching potential of the involved activities in the open comments section. Likewise, the item "The instructor(s) illustrate(s) theory by using examples from research or daily events" scored 4.7 points in the evaluation. In forthcoming years, specific questions pertaining to this initiative will be included in the evaluation form.

9. Learning outcomes

This initiative is still a work-in-progress. Although a quantitative evaluation of the learning outcomes has not yet been conducted, the students have shown a very good understanding of the involved topics as evidenced by their overall grades. The anonymized graph below (Graph 1) shows the final course grades as extracted from the grading platform of University College Utrecht.

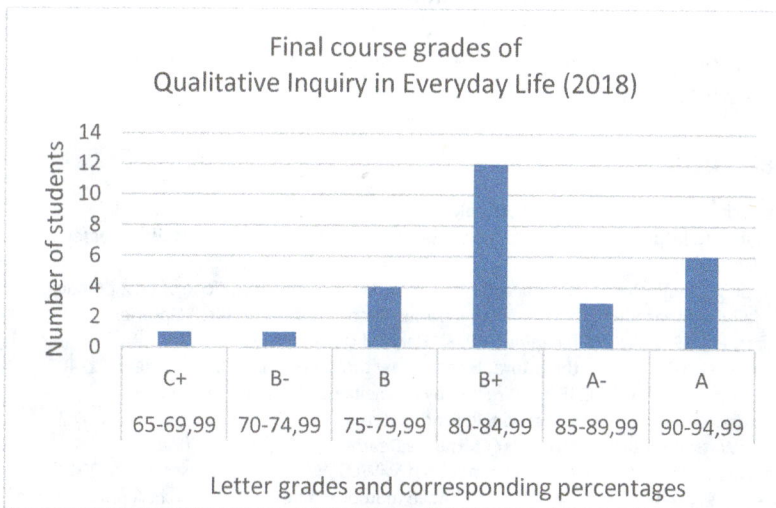

Graph 1: Anonymized student grades (Source: Osiris.uu.nl)

As per the University College Utrecht grading system, B-, B, B+ are described as "good" grades. The students who achieved these grades are deemed to have performed well i.e., in par with the expectations. The performance of students who received A- and A are considered "very good". The students, in this case, have performed above expectations.

10. Future plans for development

I am in charge of restructuring the qualitative part of the Bachelor program of Methodology & Statistics Department. The program has three yearly courses, with a capacity of 400 to 1200 students. This teaching initiative will be incorporated into the second and third courses. As a first step in this direction, some of the teaching initiative activities will be included in the forthcoming second course commencing in May 2019. The large capacity of the program makes the application of this teaching initiative quite different from that of the "Qualitative Inquiry in Everyday Life" course. Therefore, the course of May 2019 will also serve as a platform for pilot testing the initiative in a large classroom. This pilot test will mainly assess the effectiveness of 'The Circle' activity in familiarizing the topic of ethics in qualitative data collection. Additionally, I will also test the efficiency of using print commercials and magazine covers in introducing students to archival (visual, textual) qualitative data. This quantitative evaluation of the learning outcomes will be conducted in May-June 2019. Based on this experience, I will make suitable amendments to the initiative.

References

The circle synopsis. 2017. IMDb [Online].
Available at: https://www.imdb.com/title/tt4287320/plotsummary#synopsis [Accessed 31 Jan. 2019].
Adler, P. S., Aufderheide, P., Butler, B., Jaszi, P. & Andrew, W. 2012. Code of best practices in fair use for academic and research libraries. Association of Research Libraries.
Bruner, J. S. 1990. Acts of meaning (Vol. 3). Harvard University Press.
Caron, P. L. 2002. Back to the future: teaching law through stories. U. Cin. L. Rev., 71, 405.
Catch me if you can. 2002 [Film] Directed by S. Spielberg. United States: Amblin Entertainment; Parkes/MacDonald Productions.
Emma Watson Screamed After Ellar Coltrane's Death - The Circle. 2018. [Video].
Available at: http://www.youtube.com/watch?v=WLG_H9Tba9A [Accessed 4 Feb. 2019].
Eriksson, P. & Kovalainen, A. 2015. Qualitative methods in business research: A practical guide to social research, Sage.
Gudmundsdottir, S. 1991. The narrative nature of pedagogical content knowledge. In H. McEwan & K. Egan (Eds.), Narrative in Teaching, Learning, and Research. Teachers College Press, New York.

Jonassen, D. H. & Hernandez-Serrano, J. 2002. Case-based reasoning and instructional design: Using stories to support problem solving. Educational Technology Research and Development, 50, 65-77.

Kara, H. 2013. It's hard to tell how research feels: using fiction to enhance academic research and writing. Qualitative Research in Organizations and Management: An International Journal, 8, 70-84.

Limitations on exclusive rights: Fair use. 17 U.S. Code § 107.

Available at: https://www.law.cornell.edu/uscode/text/17/107 [Accessed 4 Feb. 2019].

Moezzi, M., Janda, K. B. & Rotmann, S. 2017. Using stories, narratives, and storytelling in energy and climate change research. Energy research & social science, 31, 1-10.

Nair, L.B. (In press – a). Mischief unmanaged": Approaching ethics in qualitative business research with Harry Potter. Sage Business Cases.

Nair, L.B. (In press – b). "What is Her Story?": Investigating sexual harassment in modern workplace qualitatively. Sage Business Cases.

Patel, H. (2017). The Circle (2017) - Finding Criminal Scene. [Video].

Available at: http://www.youtube.com/watch?v=Mro9RCAhvE4 [Accessed 4 Feb. 2019].

Ritchie, J., Lewis, J., Nicholls, C. M. & Ormston, R. 2013. Qualitative research practice: A guide for social science students and researchers, sage.

Saldaña, J. 2009. Popular film as an instructional strategy in qualitative research methods courses. Qualitative Inquiry, 15, 247-261.

The circle. 2017. Directed by A Bregman, G. G. A. T. H. United States: Image Nation Abu Dhabi, Playtone, Likely Story, IM Global.

Author Biography

Lakshmi Balachandran Nair is Senior Assistant Professor (Methodology and Statistics Department, Utrecht University). She has published articles, case studies, and books in a number of places including the *Journal of Business Research, Journal of Management Inquiry, Sage Publishers* etc. She has won accolades from *Swiss National Foundation, Academy of Management, Interdisciplinary Social Sciences Network, and British Academy of Management.*

Research Hacks: Navigating the 'Invisible Work' of Research

Maébh Coleman
Technological University Dublin, Ireland
maebh.coleman@dit.ie

Abstract: This case demonstrates the design and rollout of a new way of teaching Research Methods at the College of Business, Technological University Dublin using; one lecturer, 5 Research Hacks, blended learning approaches and lessons from innovation and technology management. The case raises the concept of a research methods equivalent of 'emotional labor' (Hochschild, 1983) comprising the 'invisible tasks' associated with a dissertation. This novel approach presents a method which uses user-centred design to offer a new dimension to the usual research methods curriculum predominantly through a blend of innovative assessment, directed (as opposed to self-directed) learning and explicit standards for formative and summative learning tasks.

1. Introduction

Before undertaking the development of content and assessment for the module, there were two simple objectives; that each student would:

- reach their potential, and
- have a feasible research project proposal at the end of the module.

This is not an easy task as each of these objectives are loaded with the usual challenges of teaching Research Methods (RM) and also further subjected to new and different challenges, as outlined in later sections.

A user-centred design approach was used to create a best-practice blended learning environment that would enable the prototype and development of each students' research idea into a fully feasible proposal. The assumption behind this design is that it is not necessary to develop on research proposal for assessment in an RM module and another for the 'real' research.

2. The infrastructure

The infrastructure for this module included one lecturer and the creative and efficient use of the Learning Management System (LMS), Blackboard.

There were three principles used in the design for this blended learning module:

2.1   Assessment for learning and Assessment of Learning

Formative and summative assessments were both deployed in the design of this module. Assessments to develop specific skills around the 'invisible work' were used and formatively assessed continuously throughout the module. Two key points of summative assessment were also used.

The approach to assessment included:

- 6 x regular research tasks associated with the 'invisible work' of research and assessed through the submission of regular reflective online diary entries on the task
- 4 page research brief which leveraged the work undertaken in the first half of the module and provided summative assessment
- 2 group projects which were both formative in developing research skills and summative in assessing a group output:
    - Qualitative 'mini' challenge which presents a paper to students, asks them to develop a conceptual framework and undertake research, code and analyse it to present the outcome
    - Quantitative 'mini' challenge which presents the group with the manifest of the HMS titanic and asks students to use descriptive statistics and one inferential test to explore an hypothesis
- 15 page research brief, assessed summatively, that includes the 'project management' of Level 9 research to the point of completion

2.2   Embedded Explicit Standards – Blended Delivery and Online Grading Using Rubrics

Three key benefits of effective design for blended learning were included in the design. This was because there were only 24 face-to-face teaching hours related to the course and much to learn regarding the 'hidden' work of research.

1. Scaffolding: is a concept which reduces the technical uncertainty in using technology enabled learning and provides a clear pathway for learners to reach their learning outcomes. Instructional design becomes an important element of the task for the student and for the assessor.

2. Measurability: the impact of measurability and understanding student engagement can't be underestimated. With large groups, it is possible to gain an understanding of which resources are being used, what topics are not quite understood and how students are generally getting by using the log-file data of the LMS. This contributes to general, formative feedback.

3. Efficiency in Grading and Feedback: In conjunction with the use of online rubrics, the time taken to assess and feedback on such vast amounts of student output is possible. Thus standards, grading and feedback are included in the one, online process which cuts the time taken to assess. Looking at this from a different angle, it also frees up more time for purposeful, skills-based assessments to be included in the module.

2.3   The 5 Research Hacks

The strict definition of 'Hack' is to roughly cut, chop or strike. More recently, the term is used to describe using shortcuts to accomplish goals with greater ease and efficiency then the accepted processes. These 5 Research Hacks were first trialed in small groups in 2016 and 2017 outside of TU Dublin at the Atlantic University Alliance. The hacks have been instrumental in how students understand the 'invisible work' and plan for their research as a project to enjoy rather than a sentence to be endured. They are easily accessed, low-technology techniques that used together, operate in concord to help students truly understand what they need to do and how to do it easily and efficiently. In no particular order they are:

1. Learning Diary: Regular Skill-Building Tasks Assessed Through Reflection

In the first chapter of Saunders (2011, 2015) seminal work on Research Methods for business students, there is a very important recommendation to the budding researcher which is mostly overlooked by students undertaking a dissertation. Saunders advises to use a learning diary, a multi-purpose tool for reflection and improvement. Online reflective journals are a highly effective tool and therefore it was embedded as a core element of the assessment of the module.

Students undertook structured tasks in each of the first six weeks and journalled their reflections using Gibbs (1998) reflective cycle. A small amount of in-class instruction on Gibbs model in the early weeks followed by some general feedback in weeks 3 and 4 on what students were doing right and wrong was all that was needed for this.
These entries provided a means of reflection, deep learning and internalization of the new skills, concepts and techniques that would comprise their research proposal at the end of term.

Students would not meet the required standards unless they provided regular, evidenced online entries and were graded on how they reflected the disciplined approach recommended by all writers on RM, arguably an 'invisible task'.

The entries were to:
- Screen a few dissertation ideas using Saunders feasibility indicators
- Try to make this into a research problem / goal
- Search skills and sourcing high-quality papers of relevance (citation skills and library skills)
- Research scope and context exercise
- Write 200 words on your topic using academic ton
- Create a fantasy-abstract for your final work

Students were provided with a recommended amount of 'Pomodoros' to spend, and it mostly took longer.

2. Using the Pomodoro Technique for effective time management
The Pomodoro Technique was brought up by a student in my Research Methods class in 2016 as a great way of managing time. Every task, large or small, can be broken up into smaller half-hour elements where 25 minutes is focused and purposeful and 5 minutes is total break.

Not only does this involve; self-care, time management and development of sustained focus. It also answers the key reason students become stressed during dissertation preparation, facing the mountain of 20,0000 words and not knowing what to do first. Effective task and project management for individual researchers. All tasks were explained by expressing and estimating how many 'Pomodoros' it would take.

While undertaking the 6 learning activities, students are asked to reflect on how many pomodoros it takes for them to undertake certain activities, for example write notes on a journal article or undertake a google scholar search.

The term quickly becomes a currency for the module and project planning for the research work can be confidently undertaken by having the self-awareness of how long tasks take for the individual student.

3. Absolute Requirement to Use Citation Management Software
Using proper citations is something that supervisors must demand, yet many students still try to do this by hand despite the sea-change in writing quality these tools contribute towards. A brief demonstration of how and what such tools did and how to install them and use them effectively together with a writing task brought these skills to a usable standard.

Simple tools that can prevent the loss of 10 or more marks in the grading of a dissertation for academic rigour, presentation and perhaps also high matches on Turnitin should be used when they are available.

In this module, the use of citation management software was non-negotiable, mandatory and embedded into the grading rubric. In order to demonstrate gravity to this, students who did not use the tool could not pass the module.

Challenges arose when students were tardy in implementing the use of Citation Management software in their work. When they scored less on the formative rubric, the citation behavior changed.

4. Spreadsheet framework for the critique of literature
With the reflective journaling in place to effect more internalization of learning on the module, the externalization of knowledge is also necessary.

Significant successes had been realized using commonly available models for critically analyzing literature, however rather than providing a conceptual model, recording the output in Excel-based tables somehow worked far better. Conceptual models for the critique of literature provide headings and processes to examine articles, but actually doing the critique and recording the outcomes can be problematic.

Students are intimidated by the requirement to reach 'synthesis' or 'analysis', even what is meant by 'critical analysis' and reaching this understanding is another of the 'invisible tasks' of research. Whilst researchers have developed this concept for the digital or blended environment (Churches, 2008) it has not been used for the 'invisible work' of research, such as being organized, consistent and productive.

Keeping records of what is read and the key elements of what is learned from them forms a basis for such synthesis. Over time, students can see conceptual links between different parts of their theoretical frameworks and provide new insightful synthesis and analysis using these tables as a starting point for writing. Students who demonstrate through appendices or sophisticated theoretical frameworks scored higher on the rubric.

5. Development and refinement of a theoretical framework
Another notable observation is that students generally lack the understanding of how important a conceptual framework is to the overall dissertation. In fact many institutes don't even include this as a chapter requirement of the dissertation. Notably, the Atlantic University Alliance does a highly effective job of embedding and grading the theoretical framework in their students dissertations and as a supervisor of research there for over ten years, it became clear that as soon as citation software was a requirement of writing in a small group trial, there was a notable improvement in the articulation of a theoretical framework.

The observation was that using citation management software also enables students to classify and sort the types of secondary data sources they find into a hierarchy by using a filing and categorization system. This is how a student can come to understand, or conceptualize their research topic. It is their unique mental model created from their secondary research and as such forms a basis for the theoretical framework.

The gradable element was a working model of the theoretical framework together with some operationalized variables which would direct the data collection in the final proposal.

Whether the student goes on to develop exploratory, explanatory or causal research, the will be armed with a State-of-the-art literature review to inform their goal. Care was also taken to be explicit in the definition of a theoretical gap and practice gap.

3. The challenges
There were many diverse challenges in undertaking this module. Five key issues were selected for this chapter to demonstrate the difficulties in designing, managing and assessing using the 5 hacks approach.

3.1 Challenge #1: working in a cross programmatic, cross-institutional, and multi-level module
Business Research Methods (BSRM1001) is undertaken by 7 programmes across the College of Business at TU Dublin City Campus. Students are enrolled in Level 9 taught Masters programmes with a heavily weighted dissertation element (between 20-40 ECTS) and in addition early-stage PhD researchers who seek to develop their knowledge of methodologies and research design are welcome.

2018 marked the amalgamation of three third level institutes into TU Dublin and so the studentship opened up to business students from all campuses who were forming the TU Dublin. One student was welcomed to the group from another institute.

In all there were 137 assessed students and 12 unassessed students over 7 programmes. It is a module which is cross programmatic, cross-institutional, and multi-level in its reach.

In order to tackle this challenge, a universal design approach was used to keep the learning outcomes, technology and assessments focused on the modular learning outcomes, and not programmatic level. A blend of personalization in the assessment strategy was used to fully personalize the development of research idea, yet genericize the learning outcomes through AACSB compliant rubrics, online assessments and reflective exercises.

3.2   Challenge #2 : Directed Vs Self-directed learning hours

Students did not like having all 100-120 hours designed for them. Many students in continuous assessment modules in the College of Business have face to face classes and the balance in self-directed learning hours.

However the curriculum was packed with scaffolding around the 'invisible tasks' of research design leaving no downtime at all. This surfaced in requests for extensions and for additional clarification, which was overall a relatively easy fix.

Students, knowingly and unknowingly, compare the pedagogies and assessments across their modules so it is a big ask to require such faith and commitment from them. Yet, standards and consistency provided and developed structure and trust over the course of the module. Students described having been "well-prepared" for their dissertation to their supervisors and provided feedback on the hard work being "worth it" over email

3.3   Challenge #3 Formative Vs Summative Assessment

Students are familiar with summative assessment, but not so with formative assessment. Even the most experienced educators struggle with the concept of each. Black & William (2009) furthered the conversation around formative assessment by discussing how students react to formative and summative feedback, albeit in school-based teaching scenarios. They propose that "standards can be raised only by changes that are put into direct effect by teachers and pupils in classrooms" (Black & William, 2009, p12) and in effect the main message is to lose the focus on managing grades as outcomes and focus on students reaching their potential through deep thinking and assessment for learning. During the course of the module it was patently obvious that students were overly reliant on summative assessment, 'how I scored' as opposed to working hard on what they could achieve 'potential'. Black & William discuss this concept of helping students to reach their untapped potential through formative assessment. It became very obvious as students submitted the 'research brief' a precis of their intentions. Very high potential research projects, which given the correct methods and approaches would be exceptional, were not passing as the student lacked an integration of the entire learning outcomes.

This was particularly difficult to explain to students, that the 'invisible work' of research includes slow, dedicated gradual and incremental progress toward the overall goal for a huge 20-40 ECTS project (or even more for MPhil and PhD students) rather than short, sharp and time-bounded spurts for exams and CA's associated with 5ECTS modules.

Resolution of this issue came from a blend of both formative and summative assessment, giving difficult feedback when necessary – even if this meant disappointing highly competitive students who have developed effective techniques to do well on more short-term assignments.

3.4   Challenge #4 AACSB Rubric Type Grading – Replacing the 'mark' with quality indicators

Students did not know what to do with an AACSB-type rubric feedback.

AACSB simply asks if the standard was met, not met or exceeded. While using such rubrics in an online context enabled an exceptionally high degree of personalized feedback with a high degree of speed and efficiency, there remained the issue of what to do when a student didn't meet the standards required, as occurred with the research brief many times.

It is difficult to understand how a formative rubric can tell a student they need to work harder on a specific area to do better when they have been trained to accept summative feedback without recourse to improving.

The answer to this lay again in a novel, flexible balance between formative and summative assessment. For example, in order to motivate the students to complete an idea screening research brief, the decision to award 10 marks was a good one, however, in order not to be punitive toward unknown or potential outcomes it was decided that wherever the student had fixed these issues, their final summative feedback for the proposal would be weighted at 70 rather than 60.

3.5   Challenge #5 Believe

Research Methods is a course that students and supervisors can easily dread. For students, it is a taught module that could make or break their Masters grade. For supervisors it generally resulted in a problematic relationship between early-stage research ideas and the actual feasible dissertation research projects that are carried out.

And in the middle are those who teach RM, and who for a time stand between student and supervisor in the development of knowledge and skills they need to graduate.

When significantly different methods, approaches and teaching tools are used to add new dimensions to learning, there is no template. It is exceptionally difficult to convince students to work harder than they ever have and to report to the University based on unknown metrics.

But this module really worked, and the challenge was to keep believing.

4. How the initiative was received by the users or participants

When the dust had settled, exam boards had gone ahead and supervisors were allocated I received a phonecall from a senior colleague (one whom I greatly admired) that wanted to get in touch and say this was the first time she had seen her supervisees stand before her with confidence in their chosen methodology and that they had never seen a student write paragraphs about epistemology and axiological values before. Students felt "well prepared" for the 'invisible tasks' as well as the stated requirements of the dissertation.

This feedback was also provided at several course committee meetings, a forum for staff and students to debrief on the previous semester. Therein, the feedback given was that students could now fully appreciate the amount of learning that had taken place.
Newer PhD students tended to see the entire course through to completion due to its practical value. Mid-stage PhDs tended to dip in where the course reflected their research aims.

5. The learning outcomes

Altogether there was a vast amount of work undertaken by the group as a whole. There were:
- 850 learning diary submissions
- 134 research briefs (3 students had extenuating circumstances)
- 330 group qualitative entries (33 groups)

- 330 group quantitative entires (33 groups)
- 132 research proposals

The group challenges were an outstanding success for students and really allowed them to demonstrate their skills. The outcomes were exceptionally high for these assignments and many groups exceeded the standards required. One student commented in the learning diary of the quantitative challenge:

"I felt that this was one of the more challenging assignments I have done as I always feel slightly intimidated when it comes to numbers! When Maebh was discussing quants in the lectures, I felt that it was doable but honestly, I felt a bit uneasy as its not first nature to me. However, we met as a group, discussed the task at hand in stages and it just worked from there. Also, some of the other members were strong in this area and by the end if the assignment, I feel that I could effectively implement quants in my dissertation (never thought that I'd say that!)"

Finally the research proposal again challenged the students in expanding on the feedback, but Turnitin scored demonstrated that students indeed built on their previous work, included feedback and developed the project management and data collection aspects of their proposal in the final submission. Turnitin demonstrated that approximately 40% of the content came from learning journal entries and research brief while 60% was new content.

6. Plans to further develop the initiative

BSRM1001 is now setup as a purposeful, integrated and useful module that is central to the learning pathway of many students in TU Dublin College of Business. The module is consistent, standardized and scalable. Numbers are growing with more programmes joining our ranks for the 2019 session.

In addition to the many taught Level 9 programmes that participate, the module is also being offered institution-wide for early-stage business researchers via the Research Office for September 2019.

Consideration has already been given to developing an 'after-care' suite of aids that will help with the 'invisible work' such as follow-up sessions on specific analysis tools and project managing the research.

References

Black, P., & Wiliam, D. (2009). Developing the theory of formative assessment. Educational Assessment, Evaluation and Accountability (formerly: Journal of Personnel Evaluation in Education), 21(1), 5.

Churches, A. (2008). Bloom's taxonomy blooms digitally. Tech & Learning, 1, 1-6.

Gibbs G (1988) Learning by Doing: A guide to teaching and learning methods. Further Education Unit. Oxford Polytechnic: Oxford.

Hochschild, A. R. (1983). The managed heart. Berkeley.

Saunders, M.N., 2011. Research methods for business students, 5/e. Pearson Education India.

Saunders, M., Lewis, P., & Thornhill, A. (2015). Research Methods for Business Students eBook. Pearson Australia Pty Ltd.

Author Biography

Maébh Coleman has over two decades of international business experience in government, industry and academia working with innovation-led organisations to implement technological change. She is a Teaching Fellow of TU Dublin, an e-Learning specialist and an expert in the areas of virtual communication, technology management and commerclisation processes. She currently teaches the College of Business Level 9 Research Methods module to most of its taught programmes. Her research interests include; operations management, robotics and AI, technology procurement, online service design and technology disruption.

Engaging with the Academic Literature: A Systematic Approach, Strategies and Tools

Ben K. Daniel

Educational Technology and Research Methodologies, Higher Education Development Centre, University of Otago, Dunedin 9016, New Zealand
ben.daniel@otago.ac.nz

Abstract: Engaging with the literature before data collection or theory development is a significant undertaking, critical to the development of new knowledge. However, postgraduate students and early career researchers often find it challenging to engage with the academic literature effectively. This case illustrates the development of a systematic approach and a model to support effective engagement with the academic literature. More specifically, the case presents a structure, strategies and tools to help postgraduate students and early career academics read and write credible literature reports, as well as work with a set of indicators for determining the quality of literature reports. The systematic and tripartite model was tested and evaluated with postgraduate students and early career academics (n=94) through training workshops. Those who used the tools and strategies by large found them invaluable in performing the literature review. Overall results of the evaluation were positive. Participants found the approach, structure, tools and strategies for engaging with the literature useful. They indicated that steps presented in the model eliminate the feeling that performing a literature review is daunting and that the tools for presenting credible and critical reports were helpful and easy to use. The present case is part of a research-led pedagogical initiative aimed at improving the way we approach the design and delivery of research methods in higher education.

1. Introduction to the specific objectives of the teaching initiative

Researching an academic subject, including creating new concepts and theories, requires a deep understanding of what has already been published. To obtain this knowledge requires a critical engagement with what is commonly termed as 'the literature', a task described as 'doing a literature review' (Daniel and Harland, 2018).

The literature review process and its subsequent outcome are indispensable to any scholarly work (Bradbury-Jones, Breckenridge, Clarke, Herber, Jones and Taylor, 2019), as the synthesis of existing research is key to the identification of new research questions and helps in advancing knowledge (Templier and Paré, 2015).

A literature review allows depth and breadth of knowledge to be developed in a particular subject, highlights knowledge trends, identifies existing academic debates and helps researchers frame essential research questions.

The process of the literature review is crucial to the development of the research problem and the formation of critical concepts in a study. Exploring and evaluating previous research enables the researcher to set the problem being research into the context of what is known and justify the contribution of the new research (Saunders and Rojon, 2011). Fig 1 shows that the literature is a part of every part of the research process and it is embedded in different parts of research output (e.g. thesis, research article).

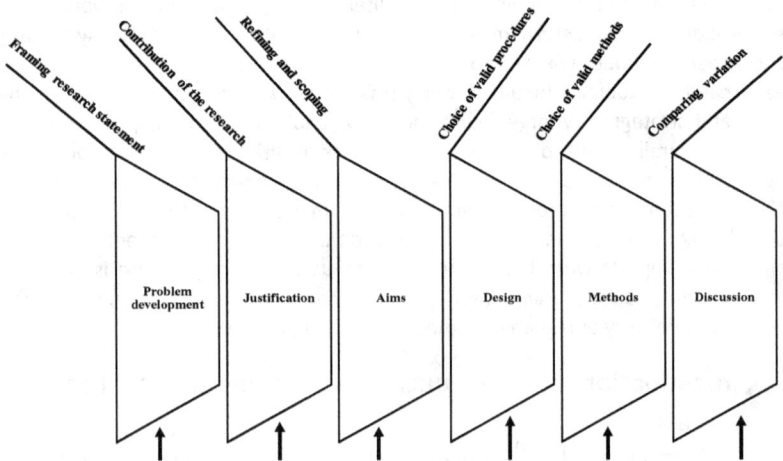

Figure 1: The role and function of academic literature

Any scholarly research that does not build on existing or previous research risks duplication of what is already known, making mistakes of others or focusing on trivial problems that do not add value to new knowledge (Terry and Terry, 2013). Our experiences of teaching research methods have clearly illustrated the difficulties students, and early career academics face when reading and critically engaging with published work (Daniel and Harland, 2018; O'Neill, Sarah and Lamb, 2018). Unfortunately, there are limited practical strategies and tools available in the literature to help students effectively undertake a literature review and efficiently write credible and critical reports (Daniel, Kumar and Omar, 2018).

In order to systematically address this problem, we asked postgraduate students in our research methods classes an open-ended question: 'what are the challenges of undertaking a literature review?' Students' responses to this question were summarised as annotations by displaying them as a Word Cloud, where more frequent words are displayed using larger font size (see Figure 2).

The visualisation of students' responses suggests that systematically approaching the literature is difficult, with organisational issues frequently mentioned. As one student noted: 'being consistent or systematic in how I organise the literature review is the biggest challenge.' An efficient way of searching and locating the literature was an issue for some students: 'time, being thorough in searching for articles, conducting the review systematically.' Also, students face challenges in writing up literature reviews: 'problems in writing in terms of coherence and linking paragraphs and doing critical analysis.' Postgraduate students also found it challenging to develop a comprehensive search strategy and systematically examine the literature and extract useful insights from the reviews. 'It is difficult to be consistent or systematic in how to search and organise the literature review, especially in interdisciplinary work where one may be working with different definitions, assumptions, and theories.'

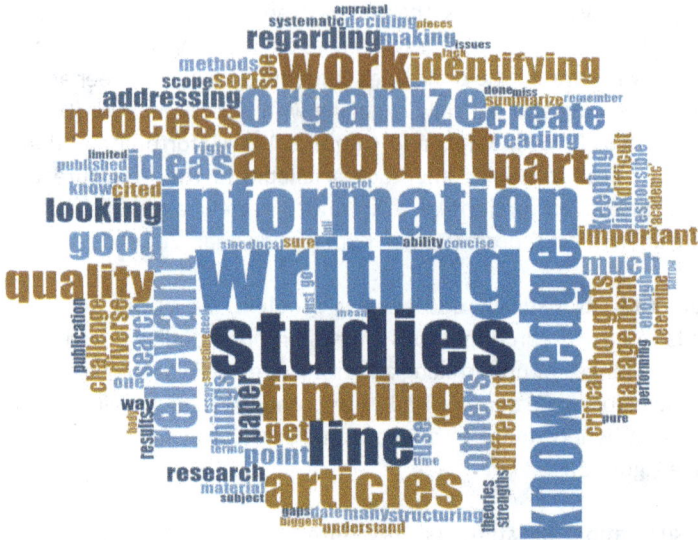

Figure 2: Summary of the Word Cloud of the challenges students face in doing literature review

Students mentioned lack of tools to help them navigate the complexity of engaging with the academic literature: 'there are no useful tools and techniques to organise the process of literature review, and how to integrate various sources of the literature into one's work.' Synthesising and critiquing the literature were identified as additional problems: 'sometimes I find it hard to understand how to link two divergent views in the literature;' 'Whenever I engage with the literature, I am certain of getting lost in the mountain of literature with difficulty in identifying what to include and exclude...;' 'I find it hard to critique weakness and strengths of the research and building an argument.' Other students reported issues of scoping the literature, or finding the relevant set of literature: 'scope – knowing when you are reading too widely or too narrowly, time management. It will be useful to know an effective way to engage the literature.' Analysis of the data revealed that students face a wide range of issues when undertaking a literature review. Figure 3 presents a summary of the seven most common challenges students face in effectively engaging with the literature.

Percentage coverage

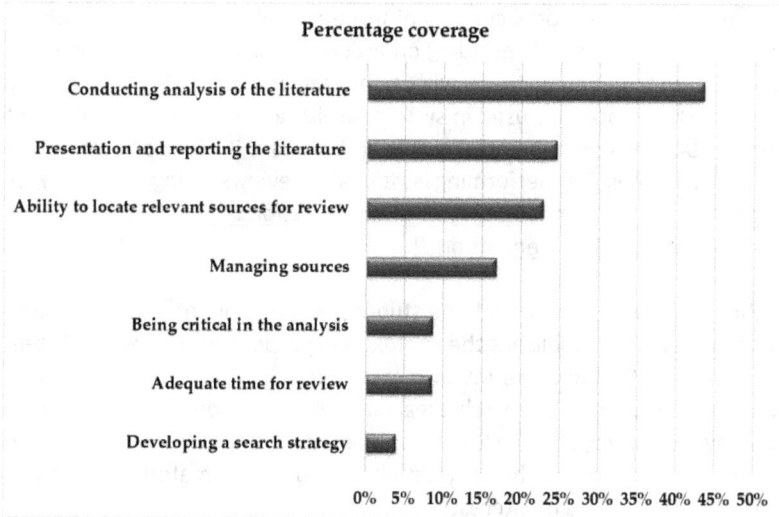

Figure 3: Seven most frequent challenges students face in engaging with the literature

2. The current case

This case history is part of an academic development programme on research methodology developed over the last five years at a public research-intensive university in New Zealand. The programme is offered to postgraduate students and early career academics in the forms of workshops and one-to-one consultations. The curriculum covers all spectrum of research methods (quantitative, qualitative and mixed methods).

Acknowledging that postgraduate students face several challenges when engaging with the academic literature, the present case focused on researching ways to answer the following questions:

- How to systematically engage with academic literature?
- How to organise credible and critical literature reports?
- How to assess the quality of literature reports?

In order to address these questions, research-informed pedagogical approach and model was developed to help students, and early career academics systematically engage with the academic literature. The model incorporates practical tools and strategies on how to write credible and critical reports. The model consists of three critical phases. The first phase of the model (Figure 4) is deciding on articles to read, compiling summary abstracts and validating these with a mentor or peer. This stage is very similar to the procedure used in systematic literature reviews (Higgins and Green, 2008; Moher, Liberati, Tetzlaff and Altman, 2009). For a complete set of guidelines for performing systematic reviews using Cochrane or PRISMA (see Cochrane https://www.cochranelibrary.com/ or PRISMA— http://www.prisma-statement.org/).

In the first stage of the model, the student begins by identifying an area of investigation and establishes the context and purpose of the review. Often, the purpose of a literature review can be directly drawn from a research statement. Framing a research area for review, and developing a search strategy, with explicit inclusion and exclusion criteria for selecting materials. This process should yield all the published material on a topic (based on the criteria of interest).

Once the purpose of the review is established, a search strategy is developed. The strategy involves the formulation of concrete search terms. It is essential to establish relevant terms since this will determine the quality of resources identified (Boell and Cecez-Kecmanovic, 2015). Students are also encouraged to consult with a subject librarian to help them develop a comprehensive search strategy. Once a search strategy is developed, students are introduced to online databases since most academic materials are indexed and archived in different online databases (e.g. Google Scholar, IEEE digital library, ACM digital library, ISI proceedings, PsycINFO, EBSCOHost, JSTOR, Cochrane Reviews, Medline, Scopus, and Web of Science).

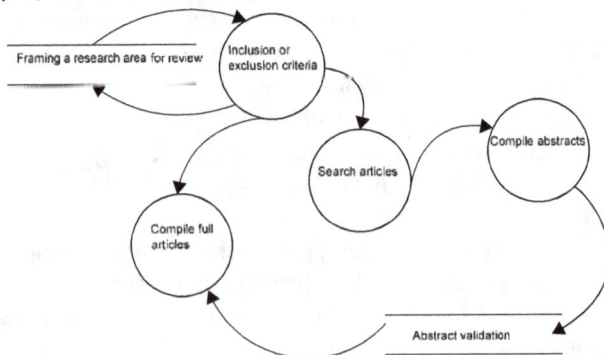

Figure 4: The stages of the systematic approach to engaging with the literature (Daniel and Harland, 2018)

Further, students are shown how to perform further searches of resources from the initial search because a database will provide a link to each article that has cited the research. Reading summaries or 'abstracts' of each article is essential. The abstracts obtained are checked against the inclusion and exclusion criteria. This is also validated against the relevance of a particular resource to the overall purpose of the review in the context of the research problem. The last part of the systematic approach involves screening and categorising published work for the review.

2.1   Review process
The second part of the model is referred to as the 'tripartite approach' because it consists of three parts and presents a model that combines the two stages as a structured and systematic guide that goes beyond reviewing the literature to how to report the findings.

2.1.1   Tripartite I (description)
In the tripartite stage (Figure 5), the systematic reviews are examined first to present a descriptive summary of the critical issues identified in the literature. This process should give the review's reader an overview of developments in the field, the main areas of debate and the outstanding research questions. The overview is usually followed by the presentation of identified themes that have been carefully justified.

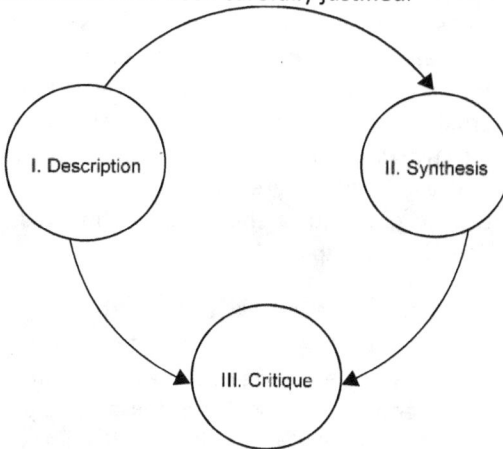

Figure 5: The Tripartite model

2.1.2   *Tripartite II (synthesis)*

A literature review goes beyond a description of what is published; it includes the synthesis and articulation of relationships between various bodies of the published literature. While literature reviews methods may vary with different types of studies, the primary purposes remain the same (Daniel and Harland, 2018). In the second part of the review process, the reviewer (student) focuses on the synthesis of ideas. To do this requires the extraction of the most important ideas or themes and a process of comparing and contrasting these to identify areas of similarity, difference and any controversies.

Synthesis of the literature allows the reviewer to clarify and resolve inconsistencies in thinking in the literature and thereby provides the best chance of making an original contribution to knowledge in the field. Through synthesis, the researcher ensures that the particular problem of interest can be contextualised within the historical context of which the subject is being studied.

2.1.3   *Tripartite III (critique)*

In the third part, the researcher reflects on the synthesis of the main ideas identified at the second stage and then develops a critical view of work reviewed in the light of claims and evidence available. It is only after thorough description and summary that a level of critical thinking and judgment can later be applied in the review and presentation. Critical engagement requires the development of particular skills and strategies, and it mainly implies having the ability to examine claims against alternative evidence or views. It also requires a questioning mind and an openness to alternative views or evidence from other sources. Critique should include a positive dimension as the researcher aims to provide new ideas and alternatives. Students are presented with various ways of critiquing an article (e.g. critiquing the nature of methods, arguments, traditions, etc.) (Saunders and Rojon, 2011).

3. The systematic and the tripartite model

The two parts of the model (Figures 4 and 5) are brought together to describe a whole process of engaging and presenting literature reports (Figure 6). The components of the model and step-by-step process provide a checklist; however, the model also provides a schematic representation of the relationship between the different parts of the model (see Figure 6).

The systematic and tripartite model provides novice as well as experience academics with a structured approach to engage with the academic literature.

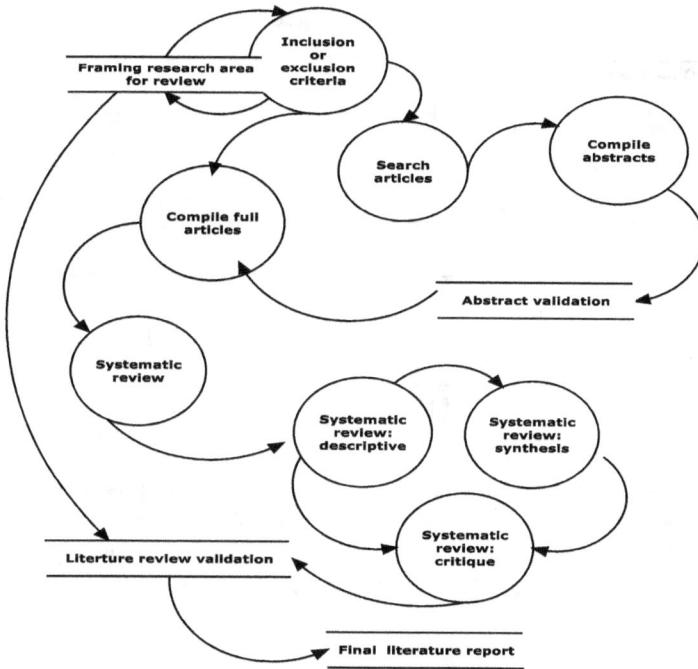

Figure 6: The systematic and tripartite approach to engage with the academic literature (Daniel and Harland, 2018)

3.1 Tools and strategies for reviewing the literature

There are two main methods to systematically examine the literature; the within-study analysis and the between-study analysis. These methods can provide an alternative to, or form part of, the tripartite model, and are used to produce a more critical and engaging report of the literature. We provide an example of how a within-study analysis can be done in the context of the tripartite model, and then provide an example of a between- study analysis that is focused on the synthesis of ideas in the literature.

Table 1: Within-study analysis

Elements reviewed	Articles reviewed				
	Article $_1$	Article $_2$	Article $_3$	Article $_4$	Article....$_n$
Aims/Objectives					
Research questions					
Methods					
Theory					
Conclusions					
Limitations					
So what?					

This type of analysis is similar to doing a peer review of a journal article or a book review. A within-study analysis begins with identifying the aims of each article, the questions raised, methods used in answering the questions, and the theory that the authors draw from, as well as the conclusions reached.

4. Between-study analysis

In contrast to the within-study procedure, a between-study literature analysis involves comparing and contrasting key findings or summaries from more than one source of literature (Onwuegbuzie and Weinbaum, 2017). When there are multiple concepts or questions to be considered in a research project, then a systematic grouping of articles can be performed.

Usually, the researcher is interested in the common concepts related to the research question and so will focus on specific article elements. In this way, an analysis can be done either 'by the group' or 'by element'. In Table 2, the focus could be on comparing all the group1 articles with group3 articles or on a synthesis of the summaries or conclusions from all groups.

Table 2: Synthesis of the articles reviewed

Elements reviewed	Articles reviewed		
	Group...$_1$(articles)	Group...$_2$(articles)	Group... $_n$(articles)
Summary			
Shared conclusions			
Contrasting views			
Current debates			
Outstanding questions			

5. Practical examples and exercises

5.1 Critical self-check questions

- Describe the research that has been done previously on your topic of interest?
- What have you learned from reviewing the literature?
- What are the dominant and minor ideas, concepts, theories and methods in what you have reviewed?
- Can you describe with illustration what the dominant theories say in the area you have reviewed?
- Are the theories compatible or incompatible with each other?
- What are your views about the theories, i.e. are there flaws in the existing literature?

5.2 Examples of common fallacies to avoid when reporting the literature

- Appeal to exaggerated research gap **(nothing is known)**
- Appeal to volume (multiple citing of unnecessary, or inconsequential work)
- Appeal to history (using historical knowledge to justify the rationale for carrying out a study)
- Appeal to emotions (soliciting credibility based on emotions)
- Appeal to authority (using the well-known figure to substantiate arguments rather than the worth of an argument)
- Appeal to fame (just because a piece of evidence is famous does not make it credible)
- Appeal to admiration (citing work based on friendship, acquaintance and respect)
- Appeal to ecological generalisation(making a conclusion at one level or

context of analysis and applying it to another)
- Appeal to multicollinearity(reaching conclusions on the grounds of two or more independent phenomena or variables)
- Appeal to a tautology (drawing conclusions on facts that true by themselves without necessarily relating them to other facts)

5.3   Example of a student using the within-study tool

Article Reviewed

Rayle, A. D., & Chung, K. Y. (2007). Revisiting first-year college students' mattering: Social support, academic stress, and the mattering experience. *Journal of College Student Retention: Research, Theory & Practice*, 9(1), 21-37.

Aims

The purpose of this study was to investigate the concept of student 'mattering' and defining it. Concepts comprise of students feeling included by their peers, feeling they were essential to the institution and feeling supported by family. This is not a novel concept, and the authors admit this in the first sentence of the abstract where they state they are revisiting a previously discussed theory from Nancy Schlossberg.

Research Questions

Does social support from friends and family predict 'mattering' to university friends and the institution? Does social support from friends and family, and mattering to university friends and the institution relate to a level of academic stress? Do male and female students differ in social support, academic stress, and mattering to university friends and the institution?

Methods

This research utilised three survey instruments, two of which were established, and the third created by one of the authors. First, the perceived social support inventory-friend scale (PSS-Fr) and family scale (PSS-Fa) assessed the perception of support from both family and friends. The Daily Hassles Index for College Stress (DHI) was then used to assess academic stress and finally, the interpersonal and General Mattering Assessment (IGMA) was used to assess the sense of mattering to others. Participants were recruited using a convenience sampling method, where all students were invited to participate. They were given time to complete the surveys during class resulting in a response rate of ~87%.

Theory

The study draws on a link between social support from both family and university friends to the perceived amount of 'mattering'. Regarding feeling included in the university environment, the most important link discovered was between the social support of friends and the university environment. These two phenomena (family and university friends) could predict academic stress levels. The more social support, and the more support from family and friends, the less likely students were to be stressed in their first year. Gender was also a strong contributor to academic stress and feelings of 'mattering'. Females felt like they mattered more to family and friends, and reported higher levels of academic stress.

Conclusions

Social support from family and friends is essential in developing a sense of belonging or 'mattering' in a university environment, but equally importantly the development of new social networks and new friends contributes to decreased levels of academic stress once at university. Females tend to feel the stresses of academic life more acutely, as they feel like they matter more to their family and social support networks. In this sense, 'mattering' has both positive and negative connotations.

Limitations
This study was limited to students from one first-year course at one university in the U.S. It only utilised established surveys, rather than surveys and interviews. These surveys will provide a limited range of views and responses.

So what?
This work builds on earlier studies, in investigating this concept of 'mattering' where it is evident that forming new relationships and social support is just as critical as having existing family and friend support. Probably the most significant contribution is in the different pressures that male and female students experience as part of their first year at university and suggestions on ways to minimise this.

6. Writing and presentation examples, and tips

6.1 An example of an 'author-centric approach' to presenting the literature

The narrative in nature: E.g., author (x) conducted an observational study and concluded that global warming is caused predominantly by human activities. Author (y) confirms this view and explicitly identified deforestation and overfishing as additional factors causing environmental degradation, etc.

6.2 Example of a concept-centric approach

Researchers in human geography and environmental sciences have linked human activities such as over farming (author1; author 2; author3), overconsumption (author 1; author 2), population growth and human longevity (author 1, author 2; author 3) to climate change. Though the link between human-oriented activities and global warming is incontestable, there is a growing literature suggesting that a combination of human and natural factors (see, for example, author1; author 3; author 4...)

6.3 Tips: Structuring a literature review report

- **Introduction**—provide a brief description of the problem, issues and scoping the problem. Provide a short description of the published work
- **The body of the literature review**—provides a detailed discussion of the literature, identify the theme, engaging debates, methods, conclusions, theories, group together similar ideas, theories and methods together. Compare and contrast key ideas and themes,
- **Conclusion**—provides a summary of the debate and critical insights, outline outstanding research problems

6.4 Example: Indicators to help students assess the quality of the literature reviews

- **Clear and organised**—clear, logical, sequential flow of thoughts
- **Logically presented**—theme, topics, engaging debates, methods, conclusions, theories
- **Descriptive and informative**—provides a summary of the debate and critical insights

•	**Critical and feedback oriented**—evaluation of sources of arguments and evidence
•	**Decisive and Authoritative**—Identification of strengths and weaknesses
•	**Conclusive**—developing a stance point about what is known, written, argued
•	**Debatable and durative** —Identifying leading issues, questions, themes, issues to be explored

7. How students received the initiative and learning outcomes

The model was translated into a 3 hours workshop where postgraduate and academic staff participated. The workshop was offered ten times to 94 participants, with 50 (53%) of whom evaluated the workshop (details of evaluations can be found in Appendices 1-5). The evaluation tool used is standardised across all teaching in the institution (see Table 3). Note that due to space limitations only a sample of student evaluation results was included in the appendix as examples.

Table 3: The evaluation questions

Questions	Rating/response
1. How valuable do you think this workshop has been for you?	**Extremely valuable 1 2 3 4 5 Not valuable at all**
2. Overall, how effective have you found the facilitation of this workshop?	**Extremely valuable 1 2 3 4 5 Not valuable at all**
3. What were the best things about this workshop for you?	-- -- ---
4. How could this workshop be improved?	

8. Evaluation and the learning outcomes

Overall, participants found the workshops as extremely valuable (87.2%), and the delivery of the workshop beneficial (87%) (Table 4). For instance, one participant commented that 'in this workshop, I have gained enormous knowledge, now I know how to develop a research topic, framing research area, developing a conceptual and theoretical framework, and efficiently performing a literature review.' Another participant said they learned more effective ways of performing literature review: the tripartite tools provide me with a clear way to navigate the complexities of doing a literature review, and presenting the review.'

Table 4: Participants and workshops ratings

Workshop	The overall value of the workshop to participants (%)	The overall quality of teaching rating (%)
Workshop 1	78	78
Workshop 2	100	75
Workshop 3	83	83
Workshop 4	100	100
Workshop 5	100	100

Students said that the model helps eliminate the feeling that performing a literature review is daunting and that the various stages provided in the model were useful, as one participant commented, 'to know about the different approaches of writing a literature review.' Others mentioned that through working with tools and strategies, they were able to gain a better understanding of the theoretical and practical knowledge for performing literature review: 'the instructor provided a very valuable framework for thinking about conducting the literature review. He rendered explicit a process that is often taken for granted in academia. He created a positive climate in the session.' Further, the workshops provided participants with clarity around the systematic and tripartite model: 'Seeing the diagrams of the systematic review and tripartite approach helped me understand the concepts involved.' Others found the facilitation of the workshops engaging: 'The systematic approach undertaken in the workshop was engaging.'

9. Summary and plans to further develop the initiative

A literature review is an essential feature of any scholarly work; it establishes a firm foundation for theoretical work and advances knowledge and scientific discovery. A review of the literature not only involves gaining new knowledge but also analytical skills that can be put to use in a broad range of contexts. In a practical sense, undertaking a literature review is necessary because without it is difficult to justify the need to undertake any research, and it would be impossible to argue for a 'gap' in the literature.

The central idea presented in the current case history is systematically engaging with the literature using structured approaches is the best way for those new to research. Our experiences of teaching research methods have clearly illustrated the difficulties this group faces when it comes to reading and engaging with published work. The systematic and tripartite model was developed to provide a structured approach to performing literature reviews.

We have used the approach to good effect, and because students and academic staff have found it useful, we have some confidence in its broader utility. In particular, we think that it will have utility for learning about all forms of literature engagement, although this claim has not been tested yet. We have also used the model in our research to help us perform critical systematic reviews (see for example Asare and Daniel, 2018; Neilson, Indratmo, Daniel and Tjandra, 2019).

Due to the wide deployment of the model, students said they could approach the literature review methodically and assess the quality of other literature reviews with high confidence. However, those who participated in the workshops suggested incorporating practical examples as one participant noted: 'perhaps some examples of good practice in the literature etc., though I thought that generally, the lecturer did a pretty good job.' Participants also mentioned the need to allow more time for hands-on activities in the workshops one participant commented; 'there was a great deal of information presented. Perhaps the workshop could be divided into two sessions, with further opportunities to explore the models presented.' Others suggested more interactive, hands-on group activities; 'small group discussion and distributing to others in the workshop. It can be a different case scenario between the group discussions to get different perspectives.' 'The instructor could have given hands-on materials. We could have tried doing with some reading materials.'

To address students' suggestions, two versions of the workshops are being developed; one will focus on an introduction to the systematic and tripartite model, and the second one will be a hands-on workshop, where students will engage in a review of 3-4 articles using the systematic and tripartite tools. The workshop will be facilitated by two lecturers to allow more time for scaffolding and hands-on and group activities.

References

Asare, S., & Daniel, B. K. (2018). Factors influencing response rates in online student evaluation systems: A systematic review approach. Journal of Interactive Learning Research, 29(2), 133-144.

Boell, S. K., & Cecez-Kecmanovic, D. (2015). On being 'systematic'in literature reviews. In Formulating Research Methods for Information Systems (pp. 48-78). Palgrave Macmillan, London.

Bradbury-Jones, C., Breckenridge, J. P., Clarke, M. T., Herber, O. R., Jones, C., & Taylor, J. (2019). Advancing the science of literature reviewing in social research: the focused mapping review and synthesis. International Journal of Social Research Methodology, 1-12.

Daniel, B., Kumar, V., & Omar, N. (2018). The postgraduate conception of research methodology: Implications for learning and teaching. International Journal of Research & Method in Education, 41(2), 220-236. doi: 10.1080/1743727X.2017.1283397

Daniel, B. K., & Harland, T. (2017). Higher education research methodology: A step-by-step guide to the research process. London, UK: Routledge, 154p.

Higgins, J. P., & Green, S. (Eds.). (2008). Cochrane handbook for systematic reviews of interventions. Retrieved on May 3rd 2019 from https://community.cochrane.org/book_pdf/764

O'Neill Dr, M. M., Sarah, R., & Lamb, J. T. (2018). Using NVivo™ for literature reviews: The eight-step pedagogy (N7+ 1). The Qualitative Report, 23(13), 21-39.

Onwuegbuzie, A. J., & Weinbaum, R. K. (2017). A Framework for Using Qualitative Comparative Analysis for the Review of the Literature. The Qualitative Report, 22(2), 359-372.

Moher, D., Liberati, A., Tetzlaff, J., & Altman, D. G. (2009). Preferred reporting items for systematic reviews and meta-analyses: the PRISMA statement. Annals of internal medicine, 151(4), 264-269.

Neilson, A., Indratmo, Daniel, B., & Tjandra, S. (2019). Systematic review of the literature on big data in the transportation domain: Concepts and applications. Big Data Research. Advance online publication. doi: 10.1016/j.bdr.2019.03.001

Rayle, A. D., & Chung, K. Y. (2007). Revisiting first-year college students' mattering: Social support, academic stress, and the mattering experience. Journal of College Student Retention: Research, Theory & Practice, 9(1), 21-37.

Schryen, G. (2015). Writing qualitative IS literature reviews—Guidelines for synthesis, interpretation and guidance of research. Communications of the AIS, 37(Art 12), 286-325.

Saunders, M. N., & Rojon, C. (2011). On the attributes of a critical literature review. Coaching: An International Journal of Theory, Research and Practice, 4(2), 156-162.

Templier, M., & Paré, G. (2015). A Framework for Guiding and Evaluating Literature Reviews. Communications of the Association for Information Systems, 37(1), 6.

Terry, MM & Terry, DR (2013). The challenges of conducting literature reviews in research: Attempting to stand on the shoulders of giants, Conducting Research in a Changing and Challenging World, Nova Science Publishers, Thao Le & Quynh Le (ed), Hauppauge, NY, pp. 33-43.

Acknowledgements

The author would like to acknowledge students and academic staff who participated in the studies leading to the development and experimentation of the Systematic and Tripartite model and tools, as well as those who have participated in the workshops and providing useful feedback. This work is supported by an Internationalisation of Curriculum Grant from the University of Otago, New Zealand.

Author Biography

Ben Kei Daniel, PhD, is Associate Professor of Educational Technology and Research Methodologies at the University of Otago, New Zealand. Ben's research investigates the quality of teaching and learning of research methodologies in academic and business settings. Also, he studies the impact of Big Data and Analytics in higher education.

Appendix 1: workshop evaluation results

6 - Students
4 - Responses
67 - % Class

Q.ID: E17013395
Date of Survey: 4-25 Apr 2017

Note: For comments questions, numbers assigned to respondents, such as 1) or 3), will be missing if they have made no comment

1	How valuable do you think this workshop has been for you?	Extremely valuable	1	2	3	4	5	Not at all valuable	NIL	Median
		Number	3	1	0	0	0		0	1.2
		Distribution 1	75%	25%	0%	0%	0%		0%	
		Distribution 2*	**100%**		**0%**		**0%**			

2	Overall, how effective have you found the facilitation of this workshop?	Very effective	1	2	3	4	5	Not at all effective	NIL	Median
		Number	1	2	1	0	0		0	2.0
		Distribution 1	25%	50%	25%	0%	0%		0%	
		Distribution 2*	**75%**		**25%**		**0%**			

3   What were the best things about this workshop for you?

1) The instructor provided a very valuable framework for thinking about conducting the literature review. He rendered explicit a process that is often taken for granted in academia. He created a positive climate in the session.

3) Seeing the diagrams of the systematic review and tripartite approach helped me understand the concepts involved

4) Dr Ben used relevant examples to explain concepts and my understanding of it became much clearer.

4   How could this workshop be improved?

1) There was a great deal of information presented. Perhaps the workshop could be divided into two sessions, with further opportunities to explore the models presented.

2) By informing students how to note important point from the literature and explaining with some real examples.

3) Explain the theory development in more detail because I was a bit confused by this

4) Collaborative group work to get more student engagement.

Appendix 2: evaluation results

			Q.ID: E17016823
20 - Students			Date of Survey: 28 Jun-12 Jul
12 - Responses			2017
60 - % Class			

Note: For comments questions, numbers assigned to respondents, such as 1) or 3), will be missing if they have made no comment

1	How valuable do you think this workshop has been for you?	Extremely valuable	1	2	3	4	5	Not at all valuable	NIL	Median
		Number	6	4	1	1	0		0	1.5
		Distribution 1	50%	33%	8%	8%	0%		0%	
		Distribution 2*	83%		8%		8%			

2	Overall, how effective have you found the facilitation of this workshop?	Very effective	1	2	3	4	5	Not at all effective	NIL	Median
		Number	5	5	1	0	1		0	1.7
		Distribution 1	42%	42%	8%	0%	8%		0%	
		Distribution 2*	83%		8%		8%			

3   What were the best things about this workshop for you?

1) Has met the expectations

2) group discussions and lecturer explanations

3) The speaker's interaction with participants and the over all structure of presentation and contents were superb.

4) Practical ways to approach research

5) Systematic approach undertaken in the workshop was really engaging.

6) Discussion with other post-grad students

7) It was a good revision session for me.

8) I could arrange my literature review step more manageable

10) Interesting, good to be challenged to think about underpinning theories pertaining to research.

11) I liked the presenter's interactions with attendees, i.e. his attempts to get us to engage with what he was teaching

12) Cyclic relation between descriptive, synthetic and analytical phases of a literature review process

4   How could this workshop be improved?

1) Not too long (probably 2 hr workshops are more effective).

3) Can't be specific but there are always room to improve.

4) Possibly too long.

7) Everything was good.

8) enlarge the room capasity

10) More chatty group

11) Perhaps some examples of good practice in the literature etc., though I thought that generally he did a pretty good job

12) By incorporating example paragraphs showing the difference between a strong review and a weak review

Appendix 3: evaluation results

11 - Students
7 - Responses
64 - % Class

Q.ID: E18020856
Date of Survey: 18 May-1 Jun
2018

Note: For comments questions, numbers assigned to respondents, such as 1) or 3), will be missing if they have made no comment

1	How valuable do you think this workshop has been for you?	Extremely valuable	1	2	3	4	5	Not at all valuable	NIL	Median
		Number	4	3	0	0	0		0	1.4
		Distribution 1	57%	43%	0%	0%	0%		0%	
		Distribution 2*	100%		0%		0%			

2	Overall, how effective have you found the facilitation of this workshop?	Very effective	1	2	3	4	5	Not at all effective	NIL	Median
		Number	3	4	0	0	0		0	1.6
		Distribution 1	43%	57%	0%	0%	0%		0%	
		Distribution 2*	100%		0%		0%			

3   What were the best things about this workshop for you?

    1) The simplification of the literature review process for capturing the key points in the articles.

    2) clear, interactive with a mix of humour. very entertaining workshop

    3) some of the concepts and important parts of the literature have been discussed and I found them very useful and interesting, like what is theoretical framework? what is conceptual framework? or the literature review table.

    4) Understand how to do a systematic review

    5) How to plan out the literature survey

4   How could this workshop be improved?

    2) practical example of a good and bad literature review and critique.

    3) it is better to print the power point contents and give them to attendees. it will help them to be engaged with the discussion and even take some notes instead of copying the whole slide on a piece of paper.

    4) The facilitator seems to be very knowledgeable and he tries to go beyond the slides, which is good to help us better understand the concepts. I wish he could speak louder and showed a bit more energy, as it's not easy for us to stay engaged for 3 hours

    5) ask the students to bring some of their own work to discuss at the workshop

Appendix 4: evaluation results

6 - Students

5 - Responses

83 - % Class

Q.ID: E18025351

Date of Survey: 20 Sep-4 Oct 2018

Note: For comments questions, numbers assigned to respondents, such as 1) or 3), will be missing if they have made no comment

1	How valuable do you think this workshop has been for you?	Extremely valuable	1	2	3	4	5	Not at all valuable	NIL	Median
		Number	5	0	0	0	0		0	1.0
		Distribution 1	100%	0%	0%	0%	0%		0%	
		Distribution 2*		100%	0%	0%				

2	Overall, how effective have you found the facilitation of this workshop?	Very effective	1	2	3	4	5	Not at all effective	NIL	Median
		Number	3	2	0	0	0		0	1.3
		Distribution 1	60%	40%	0%	0%	0%		0%	
		Distribution 2*		100%	0%	0%				

3   What were the best things about this workshop for you?

  1) The interactions

  2) It was an interactive session, I could take unlimited time for questioning

  3) The facilitator provided a lot of examples and means to operationalise the concepts.

  4) The form to code or annotate every literature

4   How could this workshop be improved?

  1) Pretty well spot on. I ahve every confidence the both the presenter aand the Unit respond to evaluation and feedback and develop the workshop accordingly.

  2) the workshop as it is will be fine

  3) More hands-on/ group activities.

  4) maybe we can have some practices/discusses

  5) Building a structure of a lit review for a chosen topic as an example.

It ain't Over 'Til it's Published: Generating a Journal Article from a Thesis or Dissertation

M.R. (Ruth) de Villiers and Annemarie Davis
School of Computing, College of Economic and Management
Unisa Sciences, Unisa, South Africa
ruth.devilliers1@gmail.com
davisa@unisa.ac.za
dvillmr1@unisa.ac.za

Abstract: It's graduation day! The research is successfully complete. Student and supervisor smile as they celebrate. Now in the next step, the work must be shared, it should contribute to the body of knowledge and inform practice. The student asks in uncertainty, "How do I start? My research methodology textbooks don't deal with writing articles!" With no new data collection required, writing an article from a dissertation or thesis may seem easier than a conventional journal article. Yet, we found that it is more complex. Such an article is not just a summary of the dissertation or the thesis. Pertinent material must be selected, an argument constructed to address the research question; and a manuscript must be designed that flows logically and is complete in itself... Postgraduate research is more than simply earning a degree even for those who do not desire academic careers. Findings from postgraduate research should be disseminated and shared! To culminate degrees by sharing research widely, the College of Economic and Management Sciences at the University of South Africa (Unisa), introduced 5-day intensive academic engagement and writing skills development for emerging researchers. These writing-for-publication workshops involve interactive seminars, discussion, dedicated writing time, and one-on-one feedback meetings with the facilitator. The complexity of publication is interrogated and simplified in a congenial environment with an informal ethos, where structured interventions are aimed at submission of a research article for peer review and eventual publication. This case history for the Innovation in Teaching of Research Methodology Excellence Awards shares practices for building research capacity. The dissemination of co-authored knowledge is a positive and supportive process for enhancing scholarship and transforming postgraduate students into authors.

Keywords: Academic writing skills development; emerging researchers; research article from dissertation; peer review; skills transfer; writing for publication

1. Introduction

Academic research and the sharing of findings are integral skills to advance knowledge and scholarship. The view of postgraduate research merely as a means of obtaining a qualification, does not do justice to the graduate, the supervisor, the institution nor academia in general. As practicing academics, we argue that postgraduate research should culminate in publications.

Research originates in a problem and a search for answers. The answer/solution should be shared in order to find application in general and expression in practice. But we also recognise that writing an article from a dissertation or thesis is much more complex than one may think. We identify with the views of Von Isenburg, Lee and Oerman (2017:167) who confirmed that publication after graduation is not trivial, especially given that many faculty lack expertise, support and time to author scholarly publications.

Another argument in favour of publishing master's and doctoral research is to develop skills in using the written word as a vital contributor to building knowledge and sharing peer-reviewed findings. We argue that the research supervisor's role is extended beyond graduation and there is a duty to guide the graduate to publish his or her research. While we recognise the challenges in writing an article from a dissertation or thesis and publication in general, we also recognise the potential value to the graduate and the research supervisor in terms of academic writing skills, publication and hopefully, citations.

Moreover, publishing from postgraduate research also offer financial incentives: Within the South African higher education funding framework, publishing in peer-reviewed accredited journals generates subsidies that can be used to further the research agenda, reinvest in research skills and contribute to university coffers. In some institutions, portions of these grants are used as personal incentives to encourage more publications.

Furthermore, publishing research contributes to promotion through academic ranks. Although financial benefits should never be the key driver, they cannot be ignored as a motive and enabler. As can be seen from this case history, the financial subsidies generated through accredited research outputs serve as the funding mechanism of this structured academic engagement and writing skills intervention.

Having acknowledged the importance of publication, we now stress the importance of developing the skills. This case history deals with structured interventions to bridge the gap between writing for examiners (dissertation and thesis) and writing for a specialist audience (journal article). Based on real interventions and activities, we reflect critically on the teaching initiative to ensure writing from and beyond the dissertation. We demystify the notion of "...the work is done, just reduce the words and publish!".

Although we recognise the body of knowledge on writing for publication (Kapp, Albertyn & Frick, 2011; Schick, Hunter, Gray, Poe & Santos, 2011; Simpson, 2012), the purpose of this case history is to describe our own experiences in developing writing-for-publication skills. Although our aim is to publish postgraduate research, we are equally focused on the academic writing skills. Our structured teaching initiative takes place over 5 days with some preparatory work ahead of the time and finalisation of the article shortly after the 5 day intervention. We write this case history from a dual position: one of the authors is the researcher/facilitator of the learning and the other author is the organiser of the initiative, who is an experienced academic and leader. This case history is based on our experiences over a 4-year period.

2. The teaching initiative

The outcome of the small group 5-day hands-on intensive academic engagement and writing skills intervention for developing and emerging researchers, is the submission of research articles to an accredited journal.

Master's graduates are recognised as developing researchers while doctoral graduates are recognised as emerging researchers. Participants may or may not be employed as academics at the institution – the qualifying criterion is for a participant to be a master's or doctoral graduate in the College of Economic and Management Sciences at Unisa. The intervention is funded from subsidy generated from accredited research outputs and the selected delegates participate in the intervention at no cost to them. The interactive intervention is facilitated by an experienced researcher who offers training, guidance and instruction on academic publishing.

3. Infrastructure

External and internal barriers prevent many researchers from writing for publication (Kapp, Albertyn & Frick, 2011:741). Planners and facilitators should be aware of such and should plan for enablers. As a precursor to this discussion, we confirm the importance of the logistics of the 5-day intervention, which can hinder or promote the intervention. Careful consideration in selecting a venue, choosing an appropriate facilitator, designing the programme and providing details upfront, are important.

Vitally, the participants should have time and space to focus solely on their research article. This calls for five days away from everyday life. In our experiences, when researchers have only one objective, the learning and growth are stronger and deeper. We notice a sense of relief and invigoration away from office tasks, household chores, family responsibilities and commuting time. We deliberately choose a workshop venue at least an hour's drive away from the office and ensure that the venue offers single accommodation with a desk and comfortable chair in the room, full catering and a dedicated venue for group sessions. This fosters concentration, commitment and focus. We require the venue to make workspace accessible 18 hours per day – to accommodate early risers and late-night workers allowing the participants to work according to their preference and habit.

Personal space is equally important – each participant has a dedicated double desk – books, reference material and computers can remain in the secure venue, contributing to a sense of ownership, purpose and belonging. While we recognise the movement towards electronic drafts, we find that printed copies of drafts enable holistic overviews and mark-ups for feedback. As such, the venue also provides printing facilities.

Participants have comfortable single accommodation in bush chalets, which support those who prefer to work in their own space at nights. While not a requirement, we witnessed monkeys, bushbuck, wildebeest, kudus and mongoose that wander by and occasionally visit the verandas – to the delight of some and the horror of others! Ultimately, a tranquil environment is deemed a necessity.

4. Call to participate

A call for participation is issued via the research supervisors to qualifying candidates, i.e. master's and doctoral graduates in the college in the preceding academic year. The call is also extended to those who have submitted their dissertations or theses for examination and are still awaiting the outcome. Participants can sign up for the intervention and are required to provide information on the planned article, the targeted journals and the co-author. As spaces are limited, the organiser reviews the participants and selects the group based on progress towards a draft article, previous participation in similar interventions and support from the research supervisor. Emerging researchers get preference over developing researchers.

5. Training and mentoring

The intervention is much more than developing academic writing skills – it is also about encouraging the academic writer. The nurturing and flexible attitude of an on-site facilitator is a cornerstone. Although the facilitator presents a daily teaching component, personal encouragement and informal one-on-one discussions contribute to building participants' confidence. The facilitator should be an experienced accredited researcher, but should also be keen to facilitate learning by working on a more basic level and avoiding overuse of academic jargon. The personal advice and reading of drafts by the facilitator support the writing process and are highly valued by participants. This plays an important role in building the confidence and ability of the academic writer. We work towards a safe space for learning: safe in terms of constructive criticism, encouragement and exposure to peer review. Since the workshop caters for developing and emerging researchers, their mentors or research supervisors are often co-authors and play an important role in feedback and personal contributions. The facilitator checks the developing drafts on-site for style, structure, readability, and golden-thread connections, while the supervisor is available via e-mail.

A key ingredient is an upfront 50% complete draft article – a work-in-progress. Although this changes and evolves during the intervention, it ensures that participants have spent time reflecting about the article and potential journals. When registering for the intervention, attendees must demonstrate readiness by indicating journals to target, the main argument, the theoretical framework, research methodology, the data sources and the implications of the research. An innovative feature is the friendly and informal Welcome Letter. We use this to whet participants' appetite for the venue and to tell them about the upfront distribution of the first presentation, which is a PowerPoint with basic tips on general Academic Writing: Style and Structure that they should use for self-evaluation to check their first draft ahead of the intervention.

6. Training material

The training content and ethos of the interventions remain basically stable, though the emphasis may change with the nature and needs of participants. Our strong teamwork comes into play, as the organiser-coordinator is always ready with sound new ideas and pertinent topics for the facilitator to incorporate in the next run of the workshop. Hence, for example, our current emphasis on the argument that should pervade the manuscript. Furthermore, the facilitator meta-learns from participants' experiences and problems.

Aspects encountered in a workshop serve as input for the next intervention and the PowerPoint presentations evolve accordingly.

There is variety in the paradigms and type of studies that our emerging researchers are tackling. Some of the doctoral graduates write sophisticated theoretical and philosophical manuscripts, such as auto-ethnographical articles and development of conceptual frameworks and models. In general, survey research via questionnaires and/or interviews is the most common data collection method, but we also encounter case studies, document analysis and econometric modelling. We would, of course, also like to see work based on more innovative research designs. In the 2019 orientation programme for newly-registered masters and doctoral students, it emerged that some were planning mixed-methods studies, action research and even design science research (unusual among business and commerce students, though common in computing research and engineering studies). The intervention and content will adjust as the research designs evolve.

An outline follows of the PowerPoint topics (indicated with italics). The formal training component takes about 8 hours in total over the 5 days involving daily interactive group sessions on academic writing for specialist audiences. Questions and enthusiastic informal contributions from participants add value for peers and facilitator alike. These sessions are interspersed with dedicated writing time coupled with hands-on feedback, guidance and support. Most participants demonstrate focused commitment to writing, and many lights burn after midnight!

As previously stated, the content of the article depends on the discipline and type of article, and there is considerable variety. We recommend a generic but customisable Structure that starts with a powerful sentence, emphasises the problem statement, and makes a convincing rationale for the work, supported by literature references.

The research question or hypothesis, underlying paradigm and philosophy, research design and methodology must be articulated, as well as the strategies of enquiry (quantitative/ qualitative /mixed-methods) and data collection and analysis methods. We encourage clear, focussed and explicit writing, logically sequenced. The manuscript should concisely, yet comprehensively answer the research question/s. The conclusion should summarise the findings, report the contributions and make recommendations.

It is important to recognise and discuss different types of studies. The presentation called Philosophies, Goals and Methods outlines empirical, theoretical, philosophical and meta-analytical research, as well as stances such as critical theory and empowerment research. We overview approaches such as design science research and participative action research, and do a flyover of various data collection methods and analysis techniques. Closely related to the type of study is Choosing the Journal. We require participants to identify three possible journals ahead of the intervention, which serves as valuable homework in terms of the presentation on choosing the journal. This choice is vital for the dissemination, discussion and application of one's contribution to knowledge and to practice. We take time to address the factors in targeting a journal – for example, journals that were referenced in the dissertation; advice of peers and supervisor; keyword searches; impact factor; length of article; theoretical or empirical; local or international.

Participants are encouraged to contribute by bringing along articles from various journals.

Publishing an Article, Presenting an Argument: The problem statement for the article might be only part of the problem addressed in the dissertation.

Similarly, the research question or argument might be only part of the original work. An argument is a connected series of statements to establish a position; a process of focussed reasoning, but some aspiring authors tend merely to extract text segments and write summaries... We offer them a useful approach:

- Turn the order around and first write the Results / Findings / Data Analysis section, which is the core of the article. Extract only the text, diagrams, tables (or parts thereof) that are directly relevant to the topic and thesis statement or research question.
- Then do a selective Literature Review to support the problem, the data collection and analysis. Similarly, the Interpretation, Discussion and Conclusion must be customised to the article's content and context. The argument should be communicated through each section, sometimes implicitly; sometimes explicitly.

The Golden Thread: The research question articulates the researcher's curiosity: "What do I want to find out?" Cohesion, continuity and consistency are required to tie it all together and good written communication is essential to inform the reader (the reviewer!). We discuss packaging content originating from different chapters of the dissertation compactly into a focused complete-in-itself journal article, by using the analogy of packing items onto labelled shelves, then refining, removing duplicates and filling gaps.

Furthermore, in the Golden Thread presentation, an evolving visualisation demonstrates the developing flow from the problem statement through the research question/objectives, the literature review, research design, data collection and analysis, results and finally interpretation and conclusions. During the one-on-one reviews of drafts with participants, the facilitator looks for these links.

Reporting, Discussing, Interpreting Results: The research question in the article might be identical to a research question from the dissertation, but it might also not be. This occurs particularly when a student is able to write more than one article from the dissertation, each relating to different objectives. The author should present only the results that are relevant to the research question/s in hand. Participants and pilot study (if such) should be briefly mentioned in reporting results. We teach researchers to present their results in a systematic structured way, appropriate to the quantitative or qualitative design, and without losing vital content. It is important to explain that new analysis might be needed for a reduced dataset.

Converting Process to Product: This session provides practical tips on checking and correcting the complete draft, which requires checking and rechecking, followed by revision. We point out the implications of adding, removing, changing or resequencing text. All threads should remain intact; the logic should flow: where material was removed, the text must maintain flow; new material must be integrated in context. Authors should identify and remove duplication.

Review criteria: On the final day, sets of criteria are provided for self-evaluation of the manuscript back at home. This personal critical review can be a rewarding exercise.

Ending at the Beginning: Finally, we discuss writing the Abstract and advise participants to do it last.

The sessions and presentation style are informal. There was a conscious decision not to portray a branded corporate-style ethos and logos, but rather to foster a friendly and relaxed environment.

The Power-Points and talks include humour and there is much laughter in the congenial atmosphere.

Several talks use real-world analogies to support recall. For example, we find that changes made during revisions, leave isolated text and break the connections. So the statement 'Going away leaves a Gap!' is used to draw attention to the pervasive problem of moving text from one section to another without contextualising both the former and the new location. In the Golden Thread talk, a skeleton is used to demonstrate structure and labelling, which should be in place at an early stage of write-up. We refer to 'skeleton in the cupboard' and suggest that in the design of the draft, 'shelves' represent section and subsection headers, where draft content can be 'packed in' as it is encountered, then 'tidied', rather than serially writing from beginning to end. As already mentioned, the Golden Thread is visualised in an interactive diagram of a developing thread that connects problem statement to research question/objectives, then on to literature review, research design, data collection and analysis, results and the conclusion.

7. Challenges

We find that the greatest challenge to workshop presenters is supporting the mind shift for moving beyond dissertations to journals, as considered in (i) and (ii). We also identify other challenges from our experiences.

1. Writing a journal article is different from writing a dissertation or thesis:
2. Writing an article based on a completed masters or doctorate is different from writing other articles.
3. New authors are insecure and lack confidence
4. The facilitator must deal with variety in participants' scholarly maturity and variety in the types of studies.

(i) The major point is that an article is different from a dissertation. It is a single cohesive document without chapters and not just a summary of the dissertation. The logic must flow and connect, and the 'storyline' should build up, communicating the argument of the article as a main message.

One initially presents a clear and unambiguous statement of the research problem or specific research questions or research hypotheses (Mouton, 2011:48). As stated earlier, these might not be the same as the research question of the dissertation or thesis. Each section of the article should be contextualised and contribute to addressing the question – formulating, motivating, constructing and concluding the argument in a focussed way that produces knowledge and also deals with counter arguments. It is possible, especially following a doctoral degree, to write more than one article, based on different objectives or sub-studies in the original work.

(ii) Articles from and beyond a dissertation or thesis require a distinct approach. Although they are based on a broader study in what we term 'the Big Book', it is important that the article should read as stand-alone research, complete in itself. It is not a simple case of sequentially copying and pasting verbatim extracts from the dissertation/thesis, then reducing.

We have adopted the pragmatic stance mentioned previously, of advising authors who struggle 'to move beyond', to start with the core! First produce the key contribution, the section on Results/Findings and their interpretation, then build the supporting structures which come before and after.

(iii) There is a lack of confidence among participants to use their own voices. The safety of hiding behind the work of others was part of the master's/doctoral journey through the literature reviews. We notice inherent fears amongst the emerging researchers: fear of plagiarising, but also fear of expressing views in their own words and fears of criticism and rejection. To overcome fear, we must build confidence within the safe space. Participants must be nurtured in writing text that 'gets outside of' the original, using own terminology to introduce, reflect and wrap up. They should build beyond the exact phrasing of the literature review and the verbatim words in their data analysis. They ask "How should I start...?" The answer is: With a strong sentence that engages informed readers. A simple suggestion: "What would you say to a colleague who asks 'What's this about?' ". We tell participants that their informal, off-the-cuff answer, uninfluenced by a formal extract, might provide some inspired text.

(iv) A challenge for the facilitator is dealing with different types of studies and academic levels. No participant should become bored or frustrated. Although many studies are empirical, articles of less-common genres, such as theoretical, computational, philosophical or conceptual, call for extended one-on-one sessions with such participants to address their unique needs.

The facilitator needs to be flexible and prepared to function beyond her own comfort zone in terms of research designs.

8. How the initiative was received by the participants
Given the tranquillity of the selected venue, the participants are keen to explore the lodge and surroundings. We organise arrival on the afternoon before the intervention to enable a managed taste of the environment. On Day 1 all excitement should be directed towards the sessions!

The participants' demeanour and commitment are impressive. The facilitator has to remind them to go for lunch! They have individual attitudes to tea time, most of them fetch something to drink and return almost immediately to their workstations to continue. When a draft or section is ready, they put it in the queue for the facilitator.

The facilitator overviews them, then has one-on-ones with writers in a separate sitting area where they discuss the feedback. As the week passes, the volume of drafts increases! Hence, a committed and experienced facilitator is an important enabler. Often, the facilitator's light burns after midnight!

We witness the success of friendly and personal engagements between the organiser and facilitator and the participants. Informal chatting, sitting with participants at meals and remembering participants' names add to the rapport between facilitator and participants. Participants should also learn to engage with research literature per se. The facilitator brings along her 'best friends' – a collection of research books for use by all.

Participants peruse them avidly, learning how to independently find research-related information.

On Day 5, participants are asked to share experiences. Based on our recollections, we share some of the feedback. The opportunity of being away from office and focusing solely on writing, accelerated progress and strengthened the quality of their work. Furthermore, participants greatly appreciated the personal meetings with the facilitator and discussion of their drafts. A number of participants felt that, although they had been to previous writing workshops, they had never had such a beneficial experience or such clear explanations. A rewarding experience for us was that, encouraged and stimulated by the intervention, some participants moved rapidly onto writing their next article.

We told them that the PowerPoints were their 'goodie-bag gift' to take away and use for future academic writing. Since they were mainly academics – some already supervising masters students and many of them expecting to supervise in future – some participants explicitly stated that they appreciated the training and mentoring moving beyond their immediate writing-for-publication needs and relating to their future careers. They could take the content and pass it forward.

Since 2016, the 5-day intensive academic engagement and writing skill development intervention has been repeated annually to a group of 12 developing and emerging researchers. To date, participants have published 25 of the articles drafted at the intervention in accredited journals. While we measure success by publication in accredited journals, we recognise the value of submitting to a journal, obtaining feedback, revising and correcting, or even resubmitting to a different journal. In cases where submissions are rejected, the experience is a norm in academia and a valuable learning curve. This real world experience of academic writing for publication is where the true value lies.

9. Learning outcomes

For the intervention we aim for a three-fold outcome: We want a near-complete article per participant at the end of the 5-days; we need confident authors who are more secure in their writing and argumentative skills, and finally, we require emerging researchers who are committed to sharing knowledge and who understand that writing for publication is a journey.

Measuring these outcomes is not easy – we can observe an increase in academic writer confidence, we can count the number of articles submitted and eventually published. But assessing commitment to scholarship and knowledge sharing is more complex. Some may claim that measurement is enabled through tracking the journals targeted and the success rate of publication in the years after the intervention. Some may argue that attempting to measure scholarship is exactly what is wrong with academia today: the desire to measure all that we do. Others may argue that a career with a research profile over time is the only true measure. For us, we want to believe that participants in the 5-day sessions take the knowledge through into their careers, refer back to the course material, reflect regularly on the writing-for-publication encounter, offer advice from own experiences and understand that research that is not published is a loss to academia.

Following up on progress beyond the workshops is a necessary evil. Participants are expected to deliver the output in return for attending the 5-day intervention. However, apart from the reporting, caring enquiries and encouragement must also be made. We acknowledge the constraints to rapid finalisation, experienced when back in everyday life with chores, workplace pressure and competing demands. As such, the organiser monitors progress to follow up and report to line managers or research supervisors, while the facilitator enquires gently and, where necessary, offers support beyond the intervention. Such support comes in various forms: an ear to listen; addressing the rebirth of fears and loss of self-confidence; encouragement to prioritise; comments or reviews of work sent through after the workshop. In addition, language support by a professional editor is provided.

10. Further development
Individuals learn at varying paces and respond to different teaching styles. Some grasp writing for publication rapidly; others may need more than one intervention. In reflecting, we consider how to further develop the intervention.

One possibility is a pre-intervention intervention! This would entail a 2-3 day session providing guidance on choosing journals, interpreting author guidelines, reading existing articles and getting a 'feel' for journal styles. At the end of such intervention, emerging researchers should have designed the structure of a planned article as a free-flow written draft.

Given that some may learn quicker than others, certain participants may benefit more from having a critical reader and coach in the writing-for-publication journey, instead of attending a further 5-day intervention.

11. Conclusion
Writing from and beyond the dissertation or thesis requires dedicated time and investment. At the end of the postgraduate journey, the view that publication is merely "the work is done, just reduce it and publish' is far from the truth. In fact, writing for publication is entirely different and requires a different skillset. This case history of an intervention in the Global South narrated our experiences – as practicing academics and as a team that organises and facilitates interventions towards scholarly writing and publication. We shared principles and practices for building research capacity and developing writing skills for novice authors and developing researchers. The dissemination of knowledge through co-authorship is a positive and supportive process for transforming postgraduate students into emerging authors and promoting scholarship for career development.

References

Kapp, CA; Albertyn, RM and Frick, BL. 2011. Writing for publication: an intervention to overcome barriers to scholarly writing. South African Journal of Higher Education. 25 (4): 741-759.

Mouton, J. 2011. How to succeed in your Master's and Doctoral Studies – A South African Guide and Resource Book. Pretoria: Van Schaik Publishers.

Schick, K., Hunter, C., Gray, L.C.; Poe, N.T. & Santos, K. 2011. Writing in action: scholarly writing groups as faculty development. Journal on Centers for Teaching and Learning. 3:43-46.

Simpson, S. 2012. The problem of graduate-level writing support: building a cross-campus graduate writing initiative. WPA: Writing Program Administration. 36 (1): 95-118.

Von Isenburg, M; Lee, LS., Oermann, MH. 2017. Writing together to Get AHEAD: an interprofessional boot camp to support scholarly writing in the health professions. Journal of the Medical Library Association. 105 (2): 167-172.

Author Biography

Ruth de Villiers was a research professor in the School of Computing at Unisa and after retirement was appointed as professor emeritus and academic associate. She continues to publish and supervise, but also undertakes research support, assisting colleagues with funding and rating applications and facilitating research workshops, particularly on academic writing.

Annemarie Davis is an Associate Professor in Strategic Management and conducted her doctoral research within the strategy-as-practice perspective. She has supervised several postgraduate research projects and favours qualitative studies. She is formally seconded to the College of Economic and Management Sciences as the Head of the Office of Graduate Studies and Research where she manages research and postgraduate matters.

Using Roleplay for the Understanding of Ethics as Part of a Development Approach to an Appropriate Research Methodology

Je'nine Horn-Lodewyk, Belinda van der Merwe and Bea van der Linde
Central University of Technology, Bloemfontein, **South Africa**
jhornlodewyk@cut.ac.za

Abstract: A researcher must be creative and able to use reflection to design an effective methodology (Attia & Edge, 2017). In turn, research methodology must be in line with ethical principles. The purpose of our research was to achieve a shift from conventional teaching of ethical principles in research methodology to an innovative development approach that could assure deeper understanding and integration of these principles. We instructed students to design and execute roleplay as a peer-assisted learning activity that was recorded on video. The students indicated that the roleplay sessions could foster a deeper understanding of ethics as part of a development approach to an appropriate research methodology. A deeper understanding of research- and medical ethics were obtained by the design of contentious non-ethical roleplay scenarios. We encourage lecturers from different fields to incorporate peer-assisted learning with roleplay activities as an engaging learning and developmental approach for modules on research methodology.

1. Introduction

As "Generation Z" students are now approaching university level education, we wanted to move beyond a passive learning environment to a teaching strategy that incorporates development of critical thinking, self-directed learning and cultural skills required for the 21st century. We wanted to challenge our students in an innovative way, and roleplay as an active learning method complied with this approach. The objective of this case was to delineate the use of an active learning approach of roleplay as a mode to teach research methodology. We wanted to improve on the students' knowledge of ethical principles to identify unethical behaviour in clinical research and medical practice by demonstrating a practical example through roleplay. The knowledge and skills acquired from this roleplay assignment could be used in future to incorporate ethical principles in research methodology for protocol writing and executing the acquisition of data. With the roleplay scenarios, we wanted to create a real learning experience that resembled an actual setting. With the students themselves being the actors bringing the experience to life, and furthermore, to encourage students to develop creativity and team work by working in groups.

We commence with a concise overview of the literature on ethical principles as part of the design of research methodology, peer-assisted learning and roleplay. This is followed by the pedagogy behind roleplay as an active learning approach. We then highlight the students' reflections and experiences of this innovative learning experience to assess the development of a diversity of skills.

2. Ethical principles as part of the design of research methodology

The need for ethical principals were recognised after World War II. Research practices performed at that time did not take into consideration the rights of humans as willing and informed participants. Ethics forms the foundation on which the research methodology of studies should be built. In 1997, the Food and Drug Administration Act (FDAMA) allowed permission for data to be generated by using diagnostic imaging modalities (Khaleel, 2017). In 2011, the FDA released draft guidance on Clinical Trial Imaging Endpoints Process Standard. Staff of a clinical trial can include a radiographer and a radiologist, therefore the professional scope of the radiographer has now been broadened and extended to become part of the research team. The South African radiography curriculum exit level outcomes require graduates to display the ability to identify, analyse and deal with complex and/or real-world problems and situations, providing evidence-based solutions and theory-driven arguments. The newly qualified radiographer must demonstrate the ability to critically analyse, synthesise and conclude an independent assessment of data (South African Qualifications Authority, 2019).

Research methodology must be designed in such a manner that the methods and procedures follow a systematic approach that will obtain the information required to test a hypothesis (Maheswari, 2013). The data acquired must be linked to the aim of the research. These methods and procedures must adhere to ethical principles and approval need to be obtained from a relevant research ethics approval committee. Academic institutions must provide students with the necessary tools to effectively be able to manage future research projects and pose minimal risks to research participants (Maheswari, 2013). Students, as future professionals, must be cognisant of ethical principles, both in their specific field of study and as part of conducting research. To develop the competencies required to perform ethical research, students must be able to design and manage different aspects of the research methodology according to international regulations (World Medical Association, 2003). When designing the research methodology, a managerial decision that extends to the ethical route that will be followed, must be made.

3. Peer-assisted learning

The application of the theory of ethical principles as part of research design and methodology, were researched by challenging students to be engaged in a peer-assisted learning activity involving the design of roleplay scenarios. Peer-assisted learning has been defined by Capstick (2004) as an open, informal, cooperative environment, in which students are able to set the agenda and raise their concerns, which is overseen by a trusted and approachable individual, and is of value in adjusting to university, understanding course material, enhancing the ability to do well in assessed work and building confidence. Erturk (2015) considered roleplay as an authentic learning activity that engages the learner and promotes active learning for deeper understanding of a complex ideology.

We designed our specific teaching and learning activity based on the rational proposed by Richard A. Wright (1987) in his work titled Human values in health care: the practice of ethics. Radiography students as health professionals need to have specific ethical and moral values (Botwe, Anim-Sampong, Obeng-Nkansah & Ampofo, 2016). In order to effectively achieve these learning outcomes, we have to provide academic support to the students in order to stimulate critical thinking and reflect about on actions relating to ethical behaviour (Pieterse, Lawrence & Friedrich-Nel, 2016). The students need to reach a level of deeper learning, understanding and cognitive thinking before a meaningful philosophical perspective can be achieved (Mattick & Bligh, 2006; Gillon, 1994). We designed the peer-assisted learning by roleplay to improve students' understanding with regard to medical ethical principles for clinical practice and research ethical principles required for clinical research.

4. Roleplay

Roleplay can be broadly defined as a form of simulation of a specific case scenario, real-world problems demonstrated in a scene, or a realistic clinical situation (Toohey, Wray, Wiechmann, Lin & Boysen-Osborn, 2016; Clapper, 2010). Students can engage as an individual by playing a specific role to make an emotional connection, or it can also be performed as team-based task. Advantages of roleplay in teaching and learning include a deeper comprehension of concepts and theories, realistic knowledge retention, foster critical thinking and enhance cognitive thinking (Clapper, 2010). Other advantages of this active learning approach include assisting the student to develop a focus on cultural diversity and the various skills needed for the 21st century workplace. Emotional experiences are important for storing an experience in memory. By becoming immersed in learning through emotions, thereby making a connection, the experience is stored in the memory and a longer retention of information is achieved.

5. Infrastructure and challenges

Our case focussed on diagnostic radiography students registered for the Research Practice II module (offered in the second year of a bachelor's degree course) at the time of the study, at a University of Technology in South Africa. Previously, the Research Practice II module was structured around a passive learning environment where boredom was reported in feedback from students. For our case, we re-designed the module and used a developmental theory employing roleplay as the primary active teaching approach. We were granted ethical approval by the Health Sciences Research Ethics Committee of the University of the Free State (HSREC number UFS-HSD2018/0628/2808). All second-year radiography students were invited to participate in the learning activity. Signed informed consent was obtained from each of the participants following an explanation and purpose of the research activity. Fifty-one students voluntarily participated in the evaluation of this active learning experience. They also consented to the data obtained from their questionnaires and videos being used for future teaching and learning activities. The students were instructed to divide themselves into groups, with a total of eighteen groups comprising 2–5 students per group. The assignment on the roleplay scenarios designed by the students included practical examples of unethical behaviour in medical- and research ethics.

The radiography students were given the opportunity for creative thinking by designing two roleplay scenario scenes in a group. The first roleplay scenario staged the scene for non-ethical practice in the clinical and/or medical health environment, and the second roleplay scenario represented non-ethical practice in clinical research. At that stage, none of the radiography students rotated to accredited, full-time clinical research facilities. Therefore, we hypothesised that the concept of roleplay as a peer-assisted learning technique posed an ideal method to facilitate deep learning and understanding of ethical principles in research methodology. The students designed and executed these roleplay scenarios by means of WhatsApp groups and structured contact time.

Prior to the roleplay activities, a 15-slide PowerPoint presentation on ethical principles was presented to the students. We also provided the students with reading material uploaded on the university's online teaching platform (Blackboard). The students were also supplied with links to the literature for reading on both research and medical ethics. WhatsApp communication was used between the facilitator and the groups. The instruction was to display authentic practical examples. The students had to write their own roleplay script, providing an opportunity for creative thinking by designing roleplay scenarios. The first roleplay scenario had to depict non-ethical practice linked to one medical ethics principle and the second roleplay scenario a non-ethical practice linked to a clinical research ethics principle. We provided the students with the same two rubrics for each of the roleplay scenarios, which assisted the students with guidance for the execution of their performances. We asked the different student groups to evaluate each other in this active learning process. This peer evaluation facilitated engagement between groups and internalisation of peer-assisted learning. Criteria on the rubric included imagination and creativity, understanding of the topics, cooperation and presentation. Video footage of the activities was recorded (Image 1) by the instructional designer of the two different roleplay scenarios at the institution.

Image 1: The students performing their medical ethics and research ethics scenarios based on non-ethical practices.

6. Student feedback

The data in this study were collected in 2019. No similar study using two different roleplay scenarios to cultivate an understanding of ethics as part of a developmental approach to research methodology, has been conducted at this particular institution. This teaching strategy employs deeper learning and the acquisition of knowledge on ethics. The roleplay indicated the understanding of ethical principles when the students could represent unethical behaviour in this manner.

In order to evaluate the experience of the students after the observation and recording of the roleplay scenarios, they were requested to complete a questionnaire that also included open-ended questions. The purpose of the questionnaire was to determine the students' opinion regarding the roleplay learning activity. They were also invited to provide a brief reflection on their own experience of peer-assisted learning as part of roleplay.

The responses were recorded by means of a 4-point Likert scale, and some items with the option to reply yes or no to specific question. The quantitative data were generated from the questionnaire that the students completed after performing roleplay scenarios on non-ethical practices linked to medical- and research ethics principles.

The majority of students (n=44; 86.3%) indicted that they liked the roleplay activities. As shown in Figure 1, a better understanding of medical ethics principles was reported by 80.4% (n=41) of students after designing a non-ethical roleplay scenario. A better understanding of research ethics was indicated by 72.5% (n=37) of the students. Of the 51 students, 44 (86.3%) indicated that they would recommend roleplay as an activity to promote peer-assisted learning for research methodology (Figure 2). Forty-four students (86.3%) were of the opinion that roleplay sessions could improve understanding of ethical principles as part of a development approach to research methodology (Figure 3).

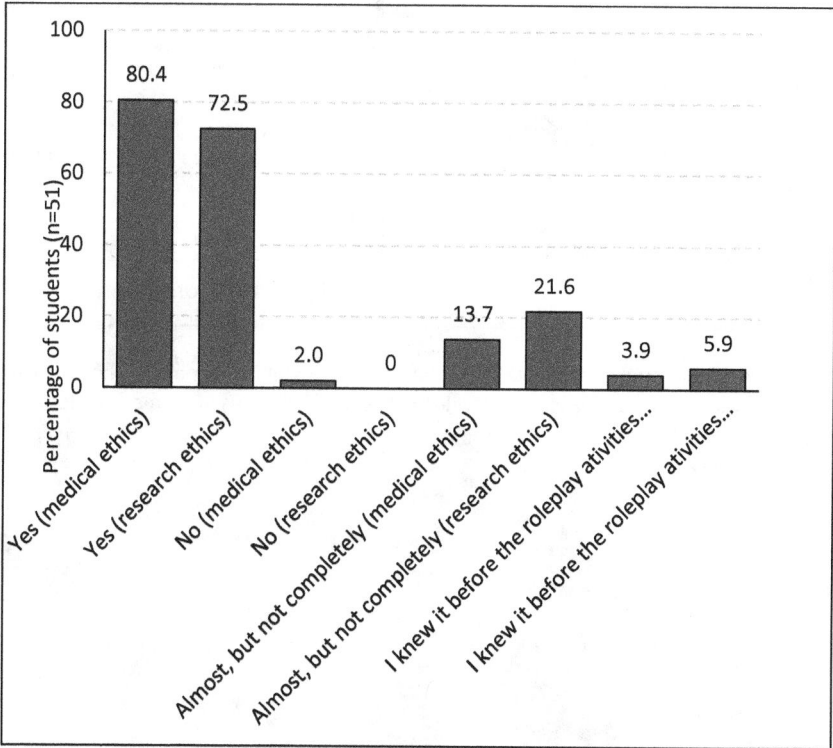

Figure 1: Students' comments on developing a better understanding of both research- and medical ethics principles after designing two non-ethical scenarios.

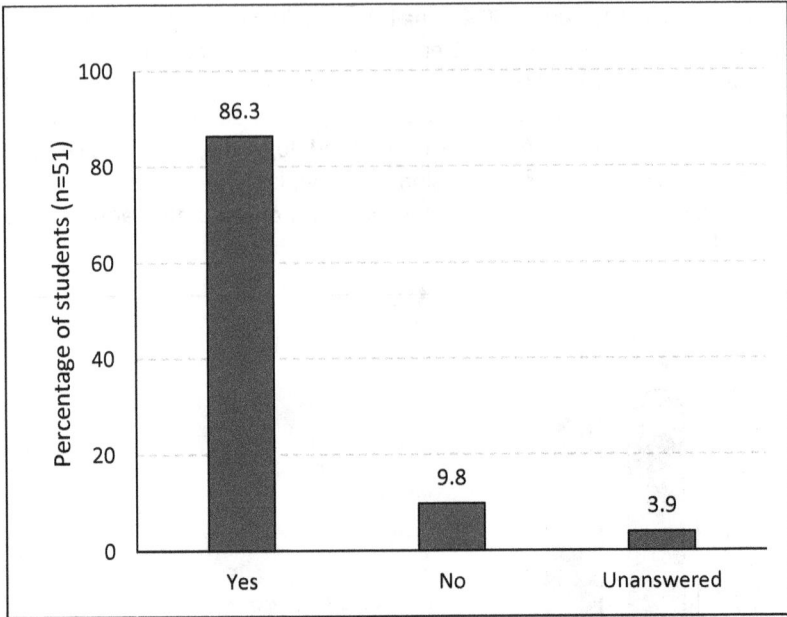

Figure 2: The students' opinion on whether they would recommend the roleplay activity as part of peer-assisted learning in the module on research methodology.

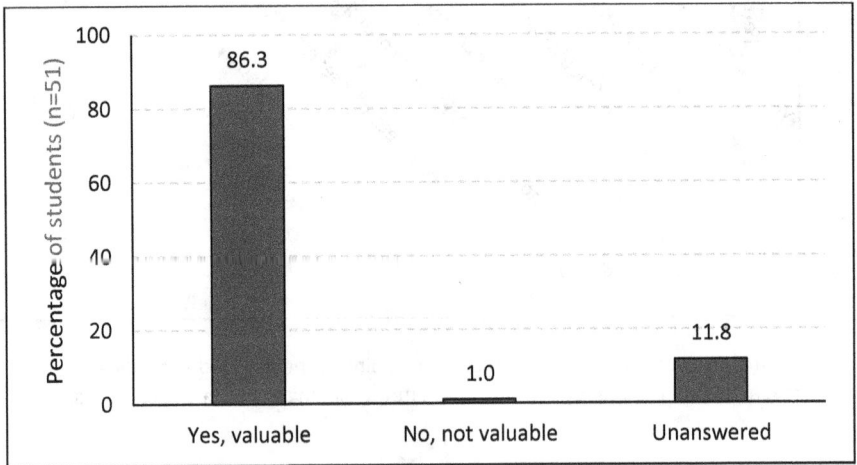

Figure 3: The students' opinion of their understanding of ethics as part of a developmental approach for research methodology.

7. Evaluation of learning outcomes

One week after the completion of the roleplay activities, students were requested to distinguish between research ethics and medical ethics. Table 1 shows some of the students' responses.

Table 1: Students' response to distinguish between research- and medical ethics (responses are shown verbatim).

Research ethics are related to the anything that is related to the research, for example the correct way of handling or working with participants when you are conducting the research. Medical ethic serves as the correct manner of handling or working patients.

The medical ethics is the code of behaviour considered to be correct at the for medical workers whilst the research ethics are the code of behaviour considered to be correct for researchers especially when conducting a study.

Research ethics is that conduct that one is required to assume when in research hence when carrying out a research project whilst medical ethics are the conduct one is expected of for instance applicable to health care workers

Research ethics are based on the ethics for the researcher to follow towards his/her research participants and Medical ethics is based on how the patients should be treated

Research ethics has to do with the participants and with the medical it is more about the patients

Research ethics are taken into consideration when a study is performed and there are people participating. Medical ethics are enforced by all medical professionals on a daily basis when working with patients.

Medical ethics is the behaviour that is considered to be correct for medical workers, research ethics is the behaviour that is considered to be correct for researchers especially when conducting a study.

Medical ethics relate to ethics that govern clinical practice and research ethics govern any time of research conducted on humans.

Research ethics are the ethical things that you should do when conducting a research like obtain informed consent from participants and medical ethics is how you should behave as a professional health practitioner when you are in practice like how you treat patients and also things you can do and not do like gossip about your patients

The difference is that research ethics relates towards researcher how the conduct their research than medical ethics it how a health care worker should conduct himself in the place of health practice.

Research ethics are principles in the analysis raised when people are as participants in a research whereas medical ethics are codes of behaviour that are considered to be correct for the members of medical profession.

Graduating radiography students are expected to apply the knowledge they have obtained from literature, as well as critically reflect on the acquired knowledge. During the roleplay activity, the students had to link each non-ethical scenario to a specific ethical principle. By giving the students the opportunity to design their own roleplay scenarios, we provided them with the opportunity to develop their creativity, communication and self-confidence. The students are no longer restricted to the conventional methods of teaching used by the department at the specific institution (Gqweta, 2012). Radiography students become absorbers of knowledge by applying through roleplay what they have learnt from the literature (Clapper, 2010). Designing their own roleplay scenarios enabled the students to question examples observed in practice, and to apply the theory of ethical principles in order to draw conclusions on what is not ethically acceptable for medical- and research practices.

The challenge posed to the facilitator was to make sure that the students understood the task correctly, as some of the ethical principles of research- and medical ethics are very similar and could be difficult to distinguish. Only one of the eighteen groups designed two scenarios based on medical ethics and not a research ethics scenario. This group found it difficult to distinguish between research- and medical ethics.

Furthermore, we experienced difficulty to obtain students' responses by means of the online tool QuestionPro, as the institutional licensing expired. Blackboard had to be used to provide the students with the reflection questionnaire and responses were analysed on this online system. A limiting factor was that the data collected were obtained at only one university, rather than various universities offering the radiography programme. The students' knowledge and application of ethical principles are complex and will only be proven if they were able to apply it in clinical practice or their own future research projects.

8. Plans to further develop the initiative

Even though ethics may be seen as a principle only applied in medicine, it is an underlying universal principle that must be applied to the research methodology of different fields, including management and engineering. The student can be provided the opportunity to design their own roleplay scenarios to facilitate a deeper understanding, interact by applying an ethical principle through creating a scenario and then reflect on what has been learnt. The peer-learning activity can provide an opportunity to identify practical examples relevant to real-life (Hicks, Lin, Robertson, Robinson & Woodrow 2001). The students' feedback we received from the open-ended and closed questions and the reflections indicated that this active learning approach was effective and successful.

We intend to take this initiative to the next level by designing a Continuous Professional Development workshop for qualified radiographers. The students gave permission to use the videos from the roleplay scenarios to assist in revising the background of radiographers on ethical principles.

References

Attia, M. and Edge, J. (2017) 'Be(com)ing a reflextive researcher: a developmental approach to research methodology' Open Review of Educational Research 4(1), 33–45.

Botwe, B.O., Anim-Sampong, S., Obeng-Nkansah, J. and Ampofo O.R. (2016) 'Ethical commitments of radiographers in a teaching hospital in West Africa: patients' perspective' The South African Radiographer 54(1), 24–27.

Capstick, S. (2004) Benefits and shortcomings of peer assisted learning (PAL) in higher education: an appraisal by students Available at: https://www.bournemouth.ac.uk/sites/default/files/asset/document/stuart-capstick.pdf [accessed 28 April 2019].

Clapper, T.C. (2010) 'Role play and simulation: returning to teaching for understanding' Education Digest 75(8), 39–43. Available at: https://eric.ed.gov/?id=EJ880890 [accessed 28 April 2019].

Erturk, E. (2015) Roleplay as a teaching strategy Available at: https://www.academia.edu/28551408/Role_Play_as_a_Teaching_Strategy [accessed 28 April 2019].

Gillon, R. (1994) 'Medical ethics: four principles plus attention to scope' British Medical Journal 309(6948), 184–188.

Gqweta, N. (2012) 'Poor academic performance: a perspective of final year diagnostic radiography students' Radiography 18(3), 212–217.

Hicks, L.K., Lin, Y., Robertson, D.W., Robinson, D.L. and Woodrow, S.I. (2001) 'Understanding the clinical dilemmas that shape medical students' ethical development: questionnaire survey and focus group study' British Medical Journal 322(7288), 709–710.

Khaleel, S.L. (2017) 'The evolution of medical imaging' Clinical Leader February 6 Available at: https://www.clinicalleader.com/doc/the-evolution-of-medical-imaging-in-clinical-research-0001 [accessed 28 April 2019].

Maheswari, Y. (2013) 'Ethics of research methodology' International Journal of Social Science and Interdisciplinary Research 2(5), 132–138.

Mattick, K. and Bligh, J. (2006) 'Teaching and assessing medical ethics: where are we now?' Journal of Medical Ethics 32(3), 181–185.

Pieterse, T., Lawrence, H. and Friedrich-Nel, H. (2016) Critical thinking ability of 3rd year radiography students Health SA Gesondheid 21(1), a995.

South African Qualifications Authority (SAQA) (2019) Registered qualification that has passed the end date: Bachelor of Diagnostic Radiography Available at: http://regqs.saqa.org.za/viewQualification.php?id=66949 [accessed 28 April 2019].

Toohey, S.L., Wray, A., Wiechmann, W., Lin, M. and Boysen-Osborn, M. (2016) 'Ten tips for engaging the millennial learner and moving an emergency medicine residency curriculum into the 21st century' Western Journal of Emergency Medicine 17(3), 337–347.

World Medical Association (2001) 'World Medical Association Declaration of Helsinki. Ethical principles for medical research involving human subjects' Bulletin of the World Health Organization 79(4), 373–374.

Wright, R.A. (1987) Human values in health care: the practice of ethics New York, NY: McGraw-Hill.

Author Biography

Dr. Je'nine Horn-Lodewyk is a radiography lecturer in the Department of Clinical Sciences at the Central University of Technology, South Africa. She facilitates a radiation physics module and research modules. Her research interests include radiopharmaceutical development, research ethics and research methodology.

Dr. Belinda van der Merwe is a senior radiography lecturer in the Department of Clinical Sciences at the Central University of Technology, South Africa. She facilitates radiographic procedure modules and work integrated learning. Her research interest include radiation safety and flexible learning.

Beatrix van der Linde is a radiography lecturer in the Department of Clinical Sciences at the Central University of Technology, South Africa. She facilitates anatomy and physiology modules. Her research interests include paediatric radiography, radiation safety and peer-assisted learning.

Using Research Informed Teaching Practices To Strengthen the Teaching and Learning of Undergraduate Research

Anisa Vahed
Dental Technology programme, Durban University of Technology, South Africa
anisav@dut.ac.za

Abstract: Undergraduate research is typified as a high-impact practice as it strengthens intellectual and practical skills; enables the practice of integrative and applied learning; and involves using advanced technologies. Research informed teaching is therefore critical in developing an understanding of the research processes at undergraduate level. More recently, Vahed and Cruickshank (2018) demonstrated that using alternate classroom based practices, such as infusing academic development and support, prepares students for the intricacies of research and the application of knowledge. In the Faculty of Health Sciences at the Durban University of Technology, academic development is structured to provide academic support and guidance to students. This is recognised in terms of the faculty having a team consisting of a dedicated Academic Development Practitioner (ADP) and Academic Development Advisors (ADAs). As outlined by the aforementioned authors, the co-teaching of the research methods and techniques subject by the ADP enhanced students' development by inculcating critical thinking and independent study skills. They therefore concluded "...the inclusion of an academic development component in the teaching of undergraduate research creates rich experiences that encourage students to succeed in research." In addition, engaging small group discussions using game based teaching, such as a Fizzer game, encourages students to reflect on their learning. This strategy of using a game to test students' understanding of their research content clarified the many areas of misunderstanding. These areas included the differences between research design, research methodology, research tools; differences between qualitative and quantitative data collection and analysis; and distinguishing between validity and reliability, amongst others. This teaching strategy facilitated the use of other techniques to scaffold the lesson by teaching core research fundamentals in smaller chunks. Essentially, instructional scaffolding in the teaching of research methods aims to progressively move students towards a stronger understanding, and ultimately, greater independence in the learning process, while experiencing how to undertake a research project.

1. Introduction to the specific objectives of the Teaching initiative

The report by the Council on Higher Education (2013: 32) emphasised that there is a dire need to increase the number of South African graduates "who are well prepared for the changing demands of society and the economy".

Recent publications by Universities South Africa (USAf), an organisation that aims to "promote a more inclusive, responsive and equitable national system of higher education" (Universities South Africa 2019), reiterated that enhancing the quality of learning and teaching on the one hand, and the quality of student experience and engagement on the other, is therefore vital (Universities South Africa 2018). A strategic pedagogical intervention to enrich student learning for them to succeed at university is to strengthen the teaching of undergraduate research, which is a high-impact practice (Kuh 2008). This supports the argument of several higher education scholars (Healey et al. 2010; Walkington et al. 2011; Spronken-Smith, Mirosa and Darrou 2013; Healey, Jenkins and Lea 2014; Walkington et al. 2018).

These scholars have widely advocated the benefits of embedding research into the undergraduate curriculum to promote skills such as problem solving, critical thinking and reflection, communication, increasing motivation and confidence, and to encourage the pursuit of postgraduate study.

Arguably, the research project at an undergraduate level requires students to adopt an autonomous role as a researcher, which is different from their previous experiences where the lecturer drives the work. As clarified in my previous study (Vahed and Cruickshank 2018) , the challenge of framing a research idea and the successive re-drafting is new for undergraduate students, especially as they are expected to make the transition to an independent mode of study. It is against this backdrop that an integrated academic development (AD) component was included in the teaching of undergraduate research. Pedagogies enabling inquiry-led learning were developed to actively engage students in the research process and for them to make the linkage to their discipline-specific practice. This aligns with Griffiths' (2004) typology of teaching-research links, specifically research-oriented and research-based teaching. Griffith (2004) explained research-oriented teaching as understanding the process by which knowledge is produced (know-why).

Teaching therefore involves using inquiry skills and on acquiring a 'research ethos'. Research-based teaching, by contrast, focuses on inquiry-based activities (know-how) rather than on the acquisition of subject content. This requires academic staff experiences and student learning activities to be highly integrated.

2. The infrastructure (i.e. people, systems, exercises, or perhaps hardware, software if any)

The 2016 (n=10); 2017 (n=10); and 2018 (n=10) cohort of students registered for the subjects 'Research Methods and Techniques I' and 'Dental Materials Science IV (Research Report)', which is part of the Bachelor of Technology (B Tech) in Dental Technology Level 4 programme at the Durban University of Technology (DUT), participated in the study. Initially, students engaged in a one-week block training session at the beginning of the year, which aimed to introduce them to the fundamental foundational knowledge on the various research discourses.

As illustrated in Table 1, the aforementioned training had an infused AD component and included training on various software such as EndNote, Black Board and Word for Thesis. Subsequently, and given the complex nature of research, academic development and support continued to supplement the teaching of undergraduate research throughout the year.

The support mainly focused on guiding students with the writing of their research proposal (Semester 1 – See Table 2) and research report (Semester 2), which required them to use a range of investigative techniques, collect and analyse data, and to graphically present, report and discuss their results/findings and conclusions. Generic skills such as time and project management were further enhanced. The following instructional scaffolding strategies were also used to enable students' access to and acquisition of research design and methodology principles and practices, amongst other research discourses.

2.1 Scaffolding research lectures by describing a concept, problem, or process in multiple ways to ensure understanding

1. Following a lecture on 'how to conduct interviews' where critical areas such as how to avoid leading questions and how to use probing techniques (Silent Probe, Echo Probe, Uh-Huh Probe), students viewed a YouTube video on the differences between a weak and a strong interview (https://www.youtube.com/watch?v=9t-_hYjAKww). Student teams using inductive methods conducted mock interviews where I observed, commented on and made suggestions for improvements. The above teaching strategy engaged students in multiple ways, which is visually, aurally and kinaesthetically. This increased their opportunities to acquire improved understanding of the concepts taught.

2.2 Discipline-specific lecturer and AD practitioner co-teaching

2. Formative assessment of students' work revealed that the literature section of the proposal was ambiguous and verbose, and lacked linkages between sentences within and between paragraphs. Students were merely summarising previous studies without linking it to their research argument. The unpacking or deconstruction of key concepts, along with the 'so what factor' was rife in their work. Hence, the co-teaching efforts of the discipline-specific lecturer and AD practitioner explained and practically demonstrated the literature review section. This was supplemented by a video titled 'Crafting an Argument' http://postgradenvironments.com/2017/09/07/crafting-an-argument/, which is licenced under Rhodes University creative commons.

2.3 Workshop interventions to enrich students learning and research experiences

3. The various workshops outlined below were conducted to enrich students' research-learning experiences by enabling them to develop transferable skills such as databases searching, managing

their reference list, and structural formatting of word documents, amongst other skills.

- EndNote, which is a reference management software used for managing bibliographies and references.
- Learning to access and use databases, which is a powerful tool aimed at widening students' search in and around their intended research.
- Writing Centre workshops to explain paraphrasing, transitions and transitional devices, amongst other fundamental writing concepts.
- Turnitin software to help students identify mistakes or weaknesses in citations so as to improve their academic writing skills, to use paraphrasing more appropriately, to gain more competence in academic literacy and apply this competence successfully to a research paper. This electronic 'text matching' tool enriches students learning experiences. Subsequently, training is supplemented by a video developed by Prof. Sioux McKenna and licenced under Rhodes University creative commons http://postgradenvironments.com/2017/09/22/misuses-turnitin-text-matching-software/
- Demonstrating the 'track-changes' function in Microsoft to enable students to effectively use the software.

The aforementioned workshops aimed to bridge the divide that has traditionally separated students and academics from closely interacting on a research level. Moreover, the knowledge and training acquired from the above workshops can help to shift the prevailing culture of undergraduate students as receivers of knowledge, towards a culture of them becoming inquirers when learning about and experiencing how to undertake their own research project.

3. The challenges

1. Students' under-preparedness in their lower undergraduate years as they lacked basic understanding on how to write academically, how to reference correctly and understand plagiarism and the implications thereof. Consequently, students perceived research to be difficult when in fact they lacked writing, reading, communication and critical thinking skills.

2. Training students on specialised software such as SPSS® Statistical software to deploy techniques of analysis. Appointing a statistician to help them better understand their results.

3. Additional cost incurred for experimental analyses, printing of A0 posters and proof reading. Subject levies were therefore reviewed and adjusted to cover the anticipated research costs.

4. How the initiative was received by the users or participants

Students conveyed that the teaching and related tasks and activities were "nurturing, helpful and constructive" as it helped "them to better grasp how to effectively read a journal article in order to extract relevant information" (Vahed and Cruickshank 2018: 571). Importantly, the inclusion of academic development as a component within their disciplinary research projects empowered them "to think critically about research writing, and subsequently to feel emancipated through the teaching process" (Vahed and Cruickshank 2018: 572). This confirms that infusing AD in the teaching of undergraduate research methods facilitates the provision of epistemological access to the ways of knowing valued by the discipline, and the university, overall. Moreover, and corroborating with Brew and Jewell (2012) and Healey and Jenkins (2018), academic development practitioners involved in research engaged learning are key agents who can initiate robust debates on undergraduate research and inquiry at departmental, faculty and institutional levels and actively contribute in the development of policies to ground undergraduate research as an educational practice in higher education institutions.

In addition, and as reported at the third International Conference on Higher education Advances (2017), the various teaching methods used helped to develop students' understandings of research (Figure 1). The positive attributes of the supervisors further contributed to a constructive and effective research-learning environment (Figure 2). Students characterised the teaching of research as the theory and the supervision of research as the practical (Vahed and Singh 2017: 226 and 227).

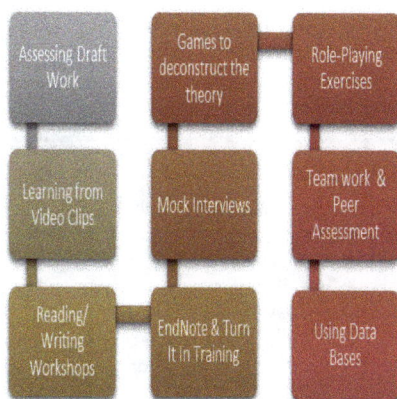

Figure 1: The various teaching practices helped develop student' understanding of

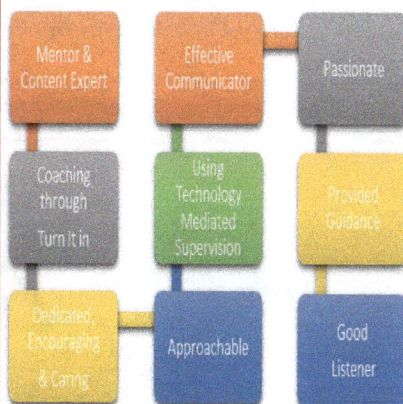

Figure 2: Positive attributes of the supervisors contributed to a constructive learning milieu.

Furthermore, students elaborated that the pedagogical strategies used enabled them to access and acquire knowledge of the various research discourses. Reportedly, they described that research supervision is the license to apply the practical knowledge of research (Vahed and Singh 2017: 227). The improved understanding of students' reported experiences have positively influenced the development of three lower-level undergraduate research modules (Levels 2, 3 and 4) for the new four-year Bachelor of Health Sciences degree in Dental Technology. This will more likely facilitate the scaling up of the research project to include a larger sample population.

Arguably, the results of the small-scale studies above have crucially foregrounded a concern, which requires deeper institutional engagements as it has implications on academic workload and performance management policies. Resonating with Brew and Jewell (2012), there is no governmental or research seed funding available for undergraduate research. This places undergraduate supervision as an additional burden on academics at Universities of Technology, who already have high teaching workloads.

5. The learning outcomes

Table 1 outlines learning outcomes achieved and the ways in which it were assessed.

Table 1: Learning Outcome for B Tech Research Subjects

1. Research Methods and Techniques 1	2. Materials Science IV- Research Report
➢ Concept Paper: Contributed 30% to the final mark. Students presented a PowerPoint to demonstrate:	➢ Research abstract: Contributed 10% to the final mark.
i. How they sourced and critically evaluated existing and relevant literature to present the context, problem statement and rationale of the study.	4. Students presented the Rationale/Objectives, Summary of work, Results, Discussion and Conclusion of their study in not more than 500 words.
ii. An understanding of the aim and objective/s of their proposed study.	
iii. Brief explanation of research design, paradigm and methodology to be followed.	
3.	
➢ Research Proposal: Contributed 70% to the final mark. The proposal is a comprehensive version of the concept paper, particularly in terms of describing conceptual and contextual understanding on qualitative research and quantitative research design and methodology. In particular, in understanding:	➢ Research Poster: Contributed 20% to the final mark. Posters presented to peers and to the wider community on DUTs Research Day.
i. Data collection and data analysis procedures.	➢ Journal Article: Contributed 70% to the final mark.
ii. Differences between validity and reliability.	
iii. Statistical analyses.]Research ethical practices.	
iv. Management of a budget.	
v. Research time management.	

6. Plans to further develop the initiative

- Renowned for her work on the ten salient practices and excellence in mentoring undergraduate research (Partridge *et al.* 2018; Walkington *et al.* 2018), Prof. Walkington and Dr Vahed are to conduct staff development workshops at DUT from the 15-26 July 2019.
- To draft the terms of reference for the teaching-research project through the office of the DVC Research, Innovation and Engagement (DUT).
- Student-supervisor learning contracts to be revised to include an explanation of 'Intellectual property' and rules of 'authorship' to publishing a paper.

Acknowledgements

Dr Gillian Cruickshank and Prof. Shalini Singh for their expertise and invaluable contributions made to the publications related to the undergraduate teaching-research nexus project.

References

Brew, A. and Jewell, E. 2012. Enhancing quality learning through experiences of research-based learning: implications for academic development. International Journal for Academic Development, 17 (1): 47-58.

Council on Higher Education. 2013. A proposal for undergraduate curriculum reform in South Africa: The case for a flexible curriculum structure. Pretoria: CHE Press.

Griffiths, R. 2004. Knowledge production and the research–teaching nexus: the case of the built environment disciplines. Studies in Higher Education, 29 (6): 709-726.

Healey, M. and Jenkins, A. 2018. The role of academic developers in embedding high-impact undergraduate research and inquiry in mainstream higher education: twenty years' reflection. International Journal for Academic Development, 23 (1): 52-64.

Healey, M., Jenkins, A. and Lea, J. 2014. Developing research-based curricula in college-based higher education York, UK: Available: https://www.heacademy.ac.uk/system/files/resources/developing_research-based_curricula_in_cbhe_14.pdf

Healey, M., Jordan, F., Pell, B. and Short, C. 2010. The research–teaching nexus: a case study of students' awareness, experiences and perceptions of research. Innovations in Education and Teaching International, 47 (2): 235-246.

Kuh, G. D. 2008. High-impact educational practices: What they are, who has access to them, and why they matter.

Partridge, L., Walkington, H., Wuetherick, B. and Moore, J. L. 2018. An international conversation about mentored undergraduate research and inquiry and academic development AU - Larson, Susan. International Journal for Academic Development, 23 (1): 6-14.

Spronken-Smith, R., Mirosa, R. and Darrou, M. 2013. Learning is an endless journey for anyone': undergraduate awareness, experiences and perceptions of the research culture in a research-intensive university. Higher Education Research & Development, 33 (2): 355-371.

Universities South Africa. 2018. Understanding Students: Putting Students at the Centre of Institutional Design. Pretoria: USAF. Available: https://www.usaf.ac.za/what-were-learning-about/ (Accessed

Universities South Africa. 2019. Welcome to USAF. Available: https://www.usaf.ac.za/ (Accessed 1 April 2019).

Vahed, A. and Cruickshank, G. 2018. Integrating academic support to develop undergraduate research in Dental Technology: A case study in a South African University of Technology. Innovations in Education and Teaching International, 55 (5): 566-574.

Vahed, A. and Singh, S. 2017. Facilitating epistemological access by developing students experiences of undergraduate research. In: València., U. P. d. ed. Proceedings of 3rd International Conference on Higher Education Advances. HEAd'17. Valencia, 21-23 June 2017. Editorial Universitat Politècnica de València, 224-230. Available: https://riunet.upv.es/bitstream/handle/10251/103925/5140-17822-1-PB.pdf?sequence=1&isAllowed=y (Accessed

Walkington, H., Griffin, A. L., Keys-Mathews, L., Metoyer, S. K., Miller, W. E., Baker, R. and France, D. 2011. Embedding Research-Based Learning Early in the Undergraduate Geography Curriculum. Journal of Geography in Higher Education, 35 (3): 315-330.

Walkington, H., Shanahan, J. O., Ackley, E. and Stewart, K. A. 2018. Mentor perspectives on the place of undergraduate research mentoring in academic identity and career development: an analysis of award winning mentors AU - Hall, Eric E. International Journal for Academic Development, 23 (1): 15-27.

Author Biography

Dr Anisa Vahed is a NRF rated researcher, HELTASA TAU Fellow, awardee of the Vice-Chancellor's Distinguished Teaching Award, DENTASA Educator of the Year Award and the HELTASA/CHE Award in Teaching Excellence. She is a senior lecturer/dental technologist in the Department of Dental Sciences at the Durban University of Technology. Her latest research project centers on the undergraduate teaching-research nexus. She has delivered papers on the above interest in a range of national and international settings.

Appendix

Table 1: Teaching and learning components of the block training in undergraduate research (Vahed and Cruickshank 2018)

TIME	DAY 1	DAY 2	DAY 3	DAY 4
08h30 - 11h55	**Interactive Session: Introduction to Research *(Section I)*** ➤ What is Research? YouTube Videos. ➤ Identification of the Research Problem. YouTube Videos ➤ Differences between an Aim/Question and Objective. ➤ Hands-on Activity: Identifying the differences between an aim and objectives. ➤ Basic Steps to a Research Project. 5. **Facilitator:** Dr Anisa Vahed	**How to Read and Summarize a Scientific Article** ➤ Reading and Scanning ➤ YouTube Videos ➤ **Hands-on Activity:** To summarise two journal articles. *(500 Word Limit)* **Facilitators:** Dr Anisa Vahed & AD Practitioner	**Literature Review *(Section II)*** ➤ General Guidelines ➤ Organisation ➤ YouTube Videos ➤ Common Errors ➤ **Hands-on Activity:** Analysing the literature review sections of research proposals. **Facilitators:** Dr Anisa Vahed & AD Practitioner	**End Note Training - *including a refresher on searching for databases*** ➤ Hands-on Activity **Facilitator:** Senior Research Librarian
12h00	LUNCH			

	Basic writing conventions: ➤ Sentence length and construction; paragraph length and construction; words not to use at the start of a sentence; bridging/linking words; phrasing within the English language; punctuation. ➤ **Plagiarism –** what it is and how to avoid it.	➤ Referencing *(Part 1)* – the DUT style of referencing: in-text and the reference list. ➤ Referencing *(Part 2) –* methods and techniques to incorporate references within the writing.	**Word Formatting for your thesis** ➤ Hands-on Activity **Facilitator:** Senior Research Librarian	**Black Board Training Linked to Research** ➤ Hands-on Activity **Facilitator:** Dr Anisa Vahed
12h35 - 15h00		**Facilitators:** Dr Anisa Vahed & AD Practitioner		
	Facilitators: Dr Anisa Vahed & AD Practitioner			

Table 2: Academic development and support with the research proposal (Vahed and Cruickshank 2018)

6. Academic Development Co-Teaching Sessions		
Research curriculum content *(Teaching components)*	**AD content** *(Co-teaching components)*	**Objectives of AD co-teaching component related to research**
	Research Proposal	
Introduction to the Research Proposal in line with DUT's requirements. **2.1 Field of Research and Provisional Title.** **2.2 Background and Context of the study.** **2.3 Problem Statement.** **2.4 Research Problem, Aim and Objectives/Research Questions.**	➤ Expectations of a literature review.	▪ To enable students to acquire knowledge on the purpose of reviewing the literature, in particular to understand what it is about and how to avoid common errors when

2.5	Scope of the Study, Limitations, Delimitations, Assumptions and Hypothesis.		conducting a literature search.
		➢ The Golden Thread of writing.	▪ To identify concepts of cohesion and flow within writing.
2.6	Literature Review.	➢ Basic writing conventions: sentence length and construction; paragraph length and construction; words not to use at the start of a sentence; bridging/linking words; phrasing within the English language; punctuation.	▪ To enable students access to, and acquisition of, knowledge on how to write within the unfamiliar discourse of research. In particular, to identify and to use their 'own voice' when writing research.
2.7	References.		
2.8	Ethics.		
		➢ Plagiarism – what it is and how to avoid it.	▪ To fully understand the ramifications of plagiarising the work of other authors.
		➢ Referencing *(Part 1)* – the DUT style of referencing: in-text and the reference list. 7. Referencing *(Part 2)* – methods and techniques to incorporate references within the writing.	▪ To enable students to understand and acquire knowledge of the DUT Harvard Reference style.